INSIGHT COMPACT GUIDE

Hong Kong

Compact Guide: Hong Kong is the ideal quick-reference guide to this amazing metropolis. It tells you all you need to know about the city's attractions, from the temples of the gods to the temples of high finance, from simple markets to sophisticated superstores, as well as wonderful cuisine and fascinating festivals.

This is one of more than 100 titles in Insight Guides' series of pocket-sized, easy-to-use guidebooks edited for the independent-minded traveller. Compact Guides are in essence travel encyclopedias in miniature, designed to be comprehensive yet portable, as well as up-to-date and authoritative.

Star Attractions

An instant reference to some of Hong Kong's most popular tourist attractions to help you on your way.

Central Market p16

Bank of China p24

View from The Peak p32

Stanley Market p36

Clock Tower p38

Nathan Road p39

Ten Thousand Buddhas p46

Lei Cheng Uk p48

Shopping streets p41

Po Lin Monastery p56

Cheung Chau harbour p58

HONG KONG

Contents

Introduction

Hong Kong – The Fragrant Harbour 5
Historical Highlights 12

Places

Route 1: Hong Kong Island: Western District 16
Route 2: Hong Kong Island: Central 22
Route 3: Hong Kong Island: Wanchai to Causeway Bay 27
Route 4: Hong Kong Island: The Peak 32
Route 5: The South of Hong Kong Island 34
Route 6: Kowloon 38
Route 7: The Eastern New Territories 44
Route 8: The Western New Territories 48
Outlying Islands:
    Lantau 53
    Cheung Chau 58
    Lamma 61

Culture

Religion and Superstition 63
Festivals and Folklore 67
Western Culture 69

Leisure

Food and Drink 71
Nightlife 77
Shopping and Markets 79

Practical Information

Getting There 83
Getting Around 84
Facts for the Visitor 87
Accommodation 93

Index 96

Hong Kong – The Fragrant Harbour

Opposite: the Star Ferry

Crossing Hong Kong harbour on the Star Ferry, it seems hard to believe that the city's name is derived from the Cantonese for 'Fragrant Harbour' – *Heung Gong*. There are a number of suggested explantions for this evocative name, but it probably derives from the trade in incense wood conducted at what is now Aberdeen – the incense trees were grown in the region around Hong Kong. Another theory ascribes the name to the bauhinia, an aromatic flower native to the region. The Hong Kong Special Administrative Region's logo is a stylised 5-petal bauhinia flower, with a star on each petal.

The terminology is, in any case, confused, as the name 'Fragrant Harbour' sometimes refers to the entire territory, and sometimes only to the island of Hong Kong, the original colony lying off the Kowloon Peninsula. The latter is also an anglicised version of the Chinese for 'Nine Dragons'. These popular mythological creatures are the benevolent inhabitants of every mountain and are also the symbol of imperialism. A legend tells of the last emperor of the Song Dynasty (960–1279), who arrived on the peninsula far from his capital after being ousted from his throne. When he remarked that he could see eight dragons – the mountains which later marked the frontier with the People's Republic of China – a court lackey remarked obsequiously that he must mean nine dragons, since he, the emperor, was also one.

The traditional and the modern

Hong Kong and China were always inseparable. When the British flag was planted on what Lord Palmerston called the 'barren island' of Hong Kong in 1841, the colony quickly became an important trading post and gateway to China. Kowloon Peninsula and Stonecutters' Island were ceded in perpetuity in 1860 and the New Territories leased to the British for 99 years in 1898. All territories reverted to Chinese sovereignty in July 1997. During the years of colonial rule, the efforts of the local, predominantly Chinese, population combined with the laissez-faire administration of the British – allowing entrepreneurs to flourish here as nowhere else on earth – have resulted in Hong Kong establishing itself as a great international trading post, a powerful centre of manufacturing and one of the world's largest financial centres.

Communist China could have repossessed Hong Kong at any time since 1949, but preferred instead to use it as a window on the Western world. Hong Kong's economy flourished as an effective export outlet for Chinese goods, which are now often manufactured under Hong Kong management on the mainland. Without the flow of Hong Kong capital and expertise, Chinese economic reforms would probably not have been able to get under way.

A local of Kowloon

Position and size

Situated between latitude 22°9' and 22°37' North and longitude 113°62' and 114°30' East, Hong Kong lies just inside the Tropic of Cancer on the same latitude as Calcutta and Havana. During the mid-19th century, the British were attracted primarily by the location of Hong Kong island which forms a natural protective shield for the deepwater harbour which to this day remains easily accessible to even the largest freight ships. The total land area of some 425sq miles (1,100sq km) is constantly being increased by land reclamation projects. Hong Kong lies off the northern delta of the Pearl River, through which traders could reach the provincial capital of Canton (present-day Guangzhou), the southern gateway to China. The harbour of Macau at the southern end of the delta, which had been in use as a trading post since the 16th century, eventually proved to be too small and too shallow, and was forced to cede its superiority to Hong Kong. Apart from the flat and sandy peninsula of Kowloon, Hong Kong is steeply mountainous. At 1,810ft (552m), Victoria Peak (*Chek Kai Shan* in Cantonese) dominates Hong Kong island, although Lantau Island has two considerably higher mountains: Lantau Peak (3,064ft/934m) and Sunset Peak (2,850ft/869m). The highest barrier in the chain of mountains in the New Territories to the north is Tai Mo Shan (3,136ft/956m).

Junks remain a common sight
Tranquillity at Shek O

Climate and vegetation

Apart from the four main areas, Hong Kong Island, Kowloon, the New Territories and the Outlying Islands (including Lantau, Lamma and Cheung Chau), most of the 235 islands that make up Hong Kong are uninhabited. Like the open countryside of the larger islands and the New Territories, they are covered by knee-high evergreen undergrowth with few trees.

Hong Kong has a subtropical climate, characterised by high temperatures and high humidity. January and February are the coolest months, with frequent mist. Then the temperatures begin to rise and visibility improves. The weather is very agreeable especially during the second half of May, the start of the hot, damp summer. Throughout the year, clothing should be light and made of natural fibres. In business situations, more formal clothes are appropriate, and expensive restaurants often refuse to admit guests dressed too casually. Even during the hottest season your luggage should include a jacket or pullover as interiors are often excessively chilly due to air conditioning.

The visitor who expects to see a concrete jungle of skyscrapers will be surprised at how green the landscape actually is. There are 23 country parks which cover some 40

Keeping up with events

percent of the surface area, not to mention the smaller, uninhabited islands. The visitor will have to search hard, however, to find the idyllic rice fields portrayed in old picture books. The population of the New Territories has been increasing steadily for years. Today, it is cheaper to import food from China than for the people to grow their own.

The flora of the region is subtropical, characterised by bamboo groves, palm trees and the odd rubber tree. Even within the city limits the occasional banyan tree has survived. The banyan (or Bo) tree, under which the Buddha achieved enlightenment, is easily recognised by its remarkable root system, often seen above ground, creeping on walls and sometimes piercing through them. Favourite decorative plants include bougainvillaea, hibiscus and orchid. Hong Kong's emblematic flower, the bauhinia, blooms in a variety of colours during autumn and is related to the orchid.

The local fauna is especially rich in insects. Shiny beetles and brightly coloured butterflies everywhere, while the chirping of cicadas is almost deafening at times. Outside the city limits, mosquitoes make the visitor's life a misery at dusk, whilst many a harmless cockroach may find its way into even the most luxurious hotel bedroom. More surprising are the large birds of prey, including black-eared kites, often seen circling above Central and other districts of Hong Kong Island.

For all this abundance of nature, the development of Hong Kong has taken little account of the natural environment: sewage and industrial waste is pumped directly into the sea, polluting the waters and making bathing potentially hazardous; the air is often thick with the unfiltered fumes of factories, power stations and cars; landscapes and marine fauna are destroyed as mountains are levelled to provide material for land reclamation.

This is not to say that there is no environmental protection in Hong Kong. The Mai Po marshes, in the extreme northwest of the New Territories, are an important conservation area; as a sanctuary for migrating birds, they are also a favourite destination for bird-watchers. Lying partly in the no-man's land between Hong Kong and China, Mai Po's future is guaranteed by international treaty. Measures are also being taken to protect the endangered pale pink-coloured Chinese White Dolphin (*Sousa chinensis*), which is under threat from water pollution and development.

Population and language

Archaeological finds on the island of Lantau and at other sites prove that the region had been inhabited, albeit very thinly, for more than 6,000 years. When the British arrived in 1841 there were a number of little fishing villages along the coast and on the larger islands. They were primarily

Hong Kong Park

Pelicans in the park

Birds in the city

the home of the Tanka, who call themselves 'Water People' because they live on their boats. The literal translation means 'Egg People', which may be due to the fact that they are purported to have paid taxes in eggs. Their origins can be traced to the Malay Peninsula, which they apparently left during the 8th century. Another group of fishermen arrived during the 18th century from the north, from what is now the Chinese province of Fujian. Their Cantonese name is Hoklo; they not only settled in present-day Hong Kong, but also migrated further to the island of Hainan and to Southeast Asia.

By the time they were leased to Hong Kong in 1898, the New Territories were more densely and evenly populated. There were no towns as such, but countless villages inhabited by peasants who worked the surrounding fields. Forty percent of the total of some 100,000 settlers were Hakka, whose home lay in the north of China but who had migrated ever further south across the centuries, arriving here during the first half of the 18th century. Women enjoy a privileged position in Hakka society, although they also work very hard physically. They are recognised by their broad-rimmed hats with black veils, and can be seen today working on the remaining fields as well as on the building sites in the city centre.

Hakka woman

From the 10th century onwards, before the arrival of the Hakka, a popular migration from other regions of China had gathered momentum. The 'Five Great Clans' – the Tang, the Hau, the Pang, the Liu and the Man – were extended families which settled the area and encouraged increasing numbers of relatives to join them. They made their homes on the best agricultural land available. The Big Five clans now number many thousands, all with the same names. They can trace their family trees back to common ancestors some 20 to 30 generations ago.

The future of Hong Kong

The present-day population of some 6.8 million is unevenly spread out. Mong Kok and the new town development of Kwun Tong (home to over 54,000 people per sq. m) are two of the world's most densely populated urban areas. Following a fire in a shanty housing estate in 1953 which destroyed the homes of some 60,000 people – most of them refugees from Communist China – the government drew up a comprehensive social housing scheme which has resulted to date in more than half of the population living in publicly subsidised housing. Over the years shopping complexes, sports halls, nursery schools, cinemas, transport facilities and other amenities have been added to the infrastructure. From the beginning of the 1980s, vast housing estates were built in the New Territories. Known as New Towns, they have replaced the old shanty towns, which have nearly been eliminated; 47 percent of the population now lives in the New Territories.

Meeting on the Promenade

Approximately 95 percent of Hong Kong's citizens are Chinese. Foreigners form a tiny minority in comparison; even during the early colonial days they never made up more than 10 percent of the population. The Filipinos represent the largest foreign contingent; some 137,500 Filipino nationals have settled in Hong Kong. The Indian minority is conspicuous along the streets, especially the tailors and the Sikh guards in front of the jewellers' shops. The Indian trading families play an important behind-the-scenes role in the local economy. Many of them arrived in Hong Kong during the 19th century from the Bombay region in the wake of British colonial trade. The makeup of the foreign population has changed in the wake of the Asian economic crisis: with 'retrenchment' leading to a 10 percent drop in the Japanese population (18,600) in 1998, and a 20 percent rise in the number of Indonesians, making them the second largest foreign group, at 44,700.

Sikh guards

The official languages in Hong Kong are English and Cantonese. Although English forms part of the curriculum in every school, only a small percentage of the population speaks the language with any degree of fluency. Local residents prefer to turn their attention to the language of mainland China, Putonghua or Mandarin Chinese. The two languages share the same written characters (although the mainland also uses a simplified version),

Night-time characters

In the street one hears virtually nothing but Cantonese; even taxi drivers and speak little or no English; policemen sometimes do, if they've been on a training course. In restaurants and hotels, however, English is usually spoken, and all official signs and documents are bilingual.

Status and administration

Hong Kong reverted to Chinese sovereignty on 1 July 1997. Under an arrangement referred to as 'One Country, Two Systems', Hong Kong is now a Special

Legislative Council building

Container port wharf

Administrative Region (HKSAR) of China, promised a high degree of autonomy. The Sino-British Joint Declaration on the future of Hong Kong, signed in 1984, stated that Hong Kong's capitalist lifestyle shall remain unchanged for 50 years after 1997; it will be free to continue its own political, social and economic systems; and will enjoy a high degree of autonomy except in foreign and defence affairs. These and other assurances were enshrined in the Basic Law, promulgated by China in 1990.

Hong Kong is governed by the HKSAR Executive Council, the main policy-making body whose chief executive is Mr Tung Chee-Hwa, and the HKSAR Legislative Assembly, which is responsible for framing legislation, enacting the laws and controlling the budget. The territory's judicial independence and the rule of law were assured by the Basic Law. However, they were seriously undermined in June 1999 when the National People's Congress in Beijing overturned a ruling by the territory's highest court, the Court of Final Appeal, that would have granted an estimated 1.67 million Mainland Chinese right of abode in Hong Kong.

The economy

Before the Asian economic crisis of 1997–99, Hong Kong was dubbed one of the 'Four Little Tigers' of Asia which demonstrated enormous economic growth and rapid industrialisation in the wake of Japan's industrial expansion after World War II. Hong Kong's beginnings were modest enough: founded as a trading post, the colony produced virtually no income as it was a free port from the start. Leasing and auctioning the small area of land available brought the government less money than it spent on infrastructure and defence. The early industries were associated with the port: shipbuilding and repairs, fishing and the supply of provisions for migrants. Trade assumed pride of place, and for a long time the scene was dominated by the two commodities which had precipitated the British annexation of Hong Kong: tea and opium).

Following the communist takeover in China in 1949, many who had cause to fear the new rulers fled the country to Hong Kong. Among them were businessmen, especially from Shanghai, which had been China's boom city during the 1920s. They invested the capital they brought with them in Hong Kong and followed Japan's example in accelerating the industrialisation process by means of simple products in the textile and plastics industries. In small factories, workers toiled virtually round the clock under unspeakable conditions for low wages. They created the East Asian economic miracle.

Hong Kong developed into a manufacturing city which, bearing in mind its small local population, was obliged to export 90 percent of its goods. The second act of the 'miracle' saw a larger range of products and a greater attention to quality. By the late 1970s, the territory was diversifying into new product development of everything from electronics to the latest fashions.

Economic and population growth increased Hong Kong's dependence on imports. The territory could not survive without food, water and energy from the mainland. After Deng Xiaoping's economic reforms in 1978, the interconnection between Hong Kong and its powerful neighbour became even closer, with Hong Kong handling a considerable proportion of Chinese exports through its trading, financial and transport infrastructure. Hong Kong's investment of vast amounts of money, staff and expertise in mainland China was reciprocated by the establishment of mainland companies in the territory and the mainland purchase of shares in Hong Kong enterprises.

Hong Kong thus evolved into a service economy. Work-intensive manufacturing industries were transferred to China's Special Economic Zones, set up in the early 1980s to stimulate rapid economic growth in strategic coastal areas without rocking socialism in the rest of China, and to other regions with low wages on the other side of the border. Although suffering from the economic downturn of October 1997–99, Hong Kong remains a major international trading and financial centre. It is the second largest stock market in Asia after Tokyo, the eighth largest banking centre, and the seventh largest foreign exchange market in the world. It is also a major transport hub; home to the world's busiest container port and one of its busiest international air cargo terminals.

HSBC headquarters

Support for the pure market economy is still virtually unanimous. The laws governing social services are minimal. Social insurance and sickness insurance have only been part of the scene for the past few years. Tax laws are very straightforward and provide the government with so much money that its reserves are growing steadily. Income and business taxes hover between 15–17 percent; capital gains are not taxed at all. But deflationary forces unleashed by the economic crisis are still at work. By May 1999 unemployment figures had risen to 6.3 percent and consumer price inflation dropped by 4 percent. Even before the recession, long working hours, minimal holidays, poor working conditions and a polluted environment were downsides to Hong Kong's economic success story.

Watching the world market

It remains to be seen how Hong Kong will weather the recession and threat to its judicial autonomy. However, comfort can be derived from the fact that, as China's main economic window on the world, it remains in China's self-interest for Hong Kong to survive and flourish as a dynamic and unfettered financial and service hub.

Historical Highlights

c 4,000BC Archaeological finds on the islands of Lamma and Lantau bear witness to scant settlement of the coastal strip.

c 1,200BC Tools and pots dating from the Bronze Age are also found. Engravings on rock surfaces also date from this era.

7th–9th century AD Apart from fishing, the settlers live by producing salt and quarrying limestone. Probable arrival of Tanka. Chinese fortress constructed in Tuen Mun.

10th–14th century Arrival of the 'Five Great Clans' in what is now the New Territories.

12th–13th century Song emperor flees south in face of Mongol invasions. Two child emperors occupy the throne from Hong Kong, but have no power.

15th–18th century Japanese and Chinese pirates maraud south Chinese coastal waters.

Early 16th century Portuguese traders are the first Europeans to reach the Canton region.

1557 Macau becomes Portuguese.

1607 Dutch and Portuguese naval forces battle off Lantau.

1700 The British establish their first 'factory' or warehouse in Canton.

1773 The East India Company unloads 150 pounds of Bengal opium at Canton

1800 Peking bans the opium drug trade, but smuggling by British traders is rife.

Early 19th century The British East India Company trading monopoly collapses. In particular, the opium trade is taken over by independent British (mostly Scottish) and American traders, for whom the British navy seeks a safe harbour. The British government hopes to open several Chinese ports to overseas trade.

1839 For economic reasons the Chinese imperial court bans the trade in opium once more, commandeering and burning the stocks in Canton. The British retaliate by shooting at Chinese guard posts, sparking off the First Opium War.

1839–41 The First Opium War. A British fleet under Captain Charles Elliot attacks Canton and takes possession of Hong Kong, without permission of the government at home.

1842 China cedes the island of Hong Kong to the British 'in perpetuity' in the Treaty of Nanjing. All Chinese governments have since refused to accept the validity of this and the following treaties as they were forced upon the Chinese and therefore 'inequitable'. Sir Henry Pottinger becomes the first governor.

1856–60 Dissatisfied with the opportunities for trade with China, the British embark on the Second Opium War and force the opening of further ports and the cession of the Kowloon Peninsula in the Convention of Peking.

1898 The British lease the region between Boundary Street in Kowloon and a range of hills to the north, as well as 233 islands (the New Territories), for a period of 99 years, i.e. until 30 June 1997.

Early 20th century A republican reform movement against the moribund imperial court of the Qing dynasty develops in south China. Sun Yatsen, who had graduated from the Chinese Medical College in Hong Kong in 1892, plays a leading role; he later becomes first President of the Republic. Since the movement is also directed against the opium trade, Hong Kong bans all opium dens. After World War I, which did not affect Hong Kong, the territory is dragged into an economic crisis by Britain.

1918 Thousands perish as fire engulfs the grandstand at Happy Valley Race Course.

1928 Mao Zedong establishes his first guerrilla base; by 1935 he has taken control of the Chinese Communist Party.

1937–45 Japanese troops attack China via Korea and precipitate a growing tide of refugees in Hong Kong. Shortly after the bombing of Pearl

Harbor in 1941, the Japanese air force destroys British aircraft at Kai Tak airport. The army advances through the New Territories and rapidly forces the defending troops to retreat to Hong Kong island, where they are forced to surrender during Christmas 1941. The Japanese army of occupation sets up concentration camps, deports workers and forces thousands to flee. Hong Kong loses one million inhabitants.

1945 At the Yalta Conference it is decided that Hong Kong should be returned to the victorious Chinese; however, the civil war which raged on the mainland until 1949 prevented this decision from being put into practice. A British military administration builds up the colony again and hands it over to a new British governor.

1950 The United Nations embargo on trade with China and North Korea during the Korean War seriously depresses the entrepôt trade, the lifeline of the colony, and conditions remain depressed for several years.

1950–3 Following the communist victory on mainland China, massive waves of refugees swell the local population. The industrialisation of Hong Kong commences.

Early 1960s Poor pay and working conditions in Hong Kong's factories lead to labour disputes and increasing social discontent.

1966–9 The Cultural Revolution in China spreads to Hong Kong via communist cells: strikes by workers and taxi drivers. Discontent reaches its climax in May 1967 when severe riots break out following a labour dispute in a plastic-flower factory. Beijing intervenes to prevent the planned general strike, thus ensuring that Hong Kong remains China's secret trade outlet.

1970 The first jumbo jet touches down at Kai Tak Airport.

1972 Richard Nixon visits China.

1975 Queen Elizabeth II becomes the first reigning British monarch to set foot in the colony.

1978 The death of Mao Zedong (1976) is followed by power struggles from which the economic reformers emerge victorious. Hong Kong's economic interconnection with China grows apace, especially following the establishment of the Special Economic Zone of Shenzen on the border. China campaigns for the return of the colony.

1979 Mass Transit Railway (MTR) opens.

1984 Following several years of negotiations, a Joint Declaration is signed by the British and Chinese governments in Beijing, making provision for the return of the entire Hong Kong territories on 1 July 1997. The capitalist economic and social systems are to be maintained for a further 50 years, but all final decisions lie in the hands of the National People's Congress in Beijing, the parliament of the People's Republic.

1987 The Hong Kong Stock Exchange crashes.

1989 Hong Kong residents take to the streets in shocked protest at the 4 June 'pro-democracy crackdown' in Tiananmen Square, Beijing.

1990 China promulgates the Basic Law (mini constitution), endorsing the aims and assurances of the Joint Declaration.

1992 A British politician, Chris Patten, replaces the career diplomats who had previously acted as governors of Hong Kong. Suggested minor changes in electoral procedures are refused by Beijing, which intends to staff the colonial administration with its own supporters.

1993–6 The Sino-British relationship deteriorates as the Chinese government spurns attempts by the British administration to introduce last-minute democratic reforms to the colony. Discussions about the practical transfer of power continue behind closed doors.

1997 Hong Kong is formally handed back to China. Tung Chee-Hwa, a shipping magnate, is appointed as the first Chief Executive at the head of a Beijing-appointed Provisional Legislature. The Hong Kong Stock Market dives on the back of the Asian economic crisis (October).

1998 First HKSAR Legco elections. Chek Lap Kok airport opens. The economic downturn continues.

1999 Unemployment reaches a 20-year high of 6.3 percent.

*Antique store on Hollywood Road
Preceding pages:
View from The Peak*

Red chillis for sale

Route 1

Hong Kong Island: Western District *See map pages 18–19*

Hong Kong is a unique city where, beneath all the skyscrapers and other temples to the burgeoning world of business and commerce, the traditional Chinese way of life still manages to thrive. Down at street level visitors can immerse themselves in the everyday life of the Far East, and there is no better way of doing this than by heading westwards on Hong Kong Island to explore the antique shops, the old temples, the flea market, the chemists, the paper shops, the rice merchants, the pawnbrokers. Wander through the market for dried foodstuffs, and on to the ginseng sorters. Take home a Chinese seal (or 'chop') with your name carved on it as a reminder of this 3-hour stroll through traditional Hong Kong, which is best taken during the afternoon when all the shops are open.

Opposite the headquarters of the Hang Seng Bank, one of the largest in the city is the **Central Market** ❶. From here, the 2,500-ft (800-m) ★ **Central–Mid-Levels Escalator** (1993), the world's longest covered outdoor escalator system, runs up to the prime residential district of Mid-Levels. Designed to relieve traffic congestion in the narrow city streets, it is switched in an uphill direction from 10.20am every morning, affording glimpses through apartment windows en route and, from the top, a bird's-eye view of the mêlée of cars and people in the alleys below.

A sharp right-hand bend with an old colonial-style police station on the left marks the start of **Hollywood Road**. The ★ **Central Police Station Compound** (1864–1925) is one of the finest examples of early colonial architecture left (not officially open to the public; but you may be allowed to look round if you report in first). Victoria Prison, behind, was built in 1841 and is still in use.

Chinese culture will be of more interest here, however, for the windows of the shops along Hollywood Road are filled with antiques galore. There are tiny snuff containers painted on the inside, every imaginable item of porcelain: dishes, plates, bowls, vases, statues and other decorative figures, furniture of every kind and, of course, temple statues from the tiny God of Literature to bronze Buddhas. Buyers should be aware that not all items on display are genuine, and prices are often exorbitantly high. According to Chinese tradition, even a copy can be a very valuable object, but at present the market is being flooded not only with the booty of grave robbers, but also with cheap imitations from China. Even certificates of authenticity are falsified with great regularity.

Hollywood Road used to be lined with three- and four-storey houses, but these are gradually being demolished to make way for new high-rise blocks. The ★★ **Man Mo Temple** ❷ marks the return to old Hong Kong. It was built in around 1842 by the notorious pirate Cheung Po-tsai after he abandoned his old way of life and entered government service. It is dedicated to Man, the God of Literature, who is revered by academics and officials, and Mo, the God of War, who attracts large numbers of policemen, pawnbrokers and antique dealers. The statues of the 10 kings of heaven guard the entrance. On the side wall are litters in which the statues are borne through the streets during the temple festival. Man wears a green garment and carries a calligrapher's brush. Mo wears a red garment and holds an executioner's sword. The altar on the left is dedicated to the black-faced god of justice, Bao Gong; that on the right to the city deity, Shing Wong. The air inside the temple is heavy with incense.

Worshipping at Man Mo Temple

Straight after the temple on the left **Ladder Street** ❸ climbs up the hill. The name 'street' is actually an exaggeration, but 'ladder' is appropriate enough. Today, the steps are concreted, but it is not hard to imagine two skinny coolies toiling up under the burden of a portly European in a sedan chair in times of yore.

Ladder Street leads up to the ★ **Museum of Medical Sciences** (Tuesday to Saturday 10am to 5pm; Sunday and some public holidays 1pm to 5pm) — a fascinating collection of traditional Chinese and modern Western medicine housed in an old Pathological Institute (1905) on Caine Lane. Back down at Hollywood Road, Ladder Street leads to ★★ **Cat Street**, whose name, however, will not be found on any town plan. The official name is Upper Lascar Row, and the nickname may refer to the cat burglars who sold their stolen goods here. Some also say that the street gained its name because the Chinese equivalent of a flea market is a 'mouse market' and the purchasers, therefore, are the 'cats'. Upper Lascar Row was once the heart of a crowded ghetto, and antiques and second-hand goods have been traded here for 150 years. During the afternoon, elderly men spread out mats and rugs on the ground in order to display their wares: amulets, jade, watches and other bric-a-brac. Some traders have proper stalls with a wider range of goods, and the street is also lined with antique and furniture shops.

Hollywood Road antiques

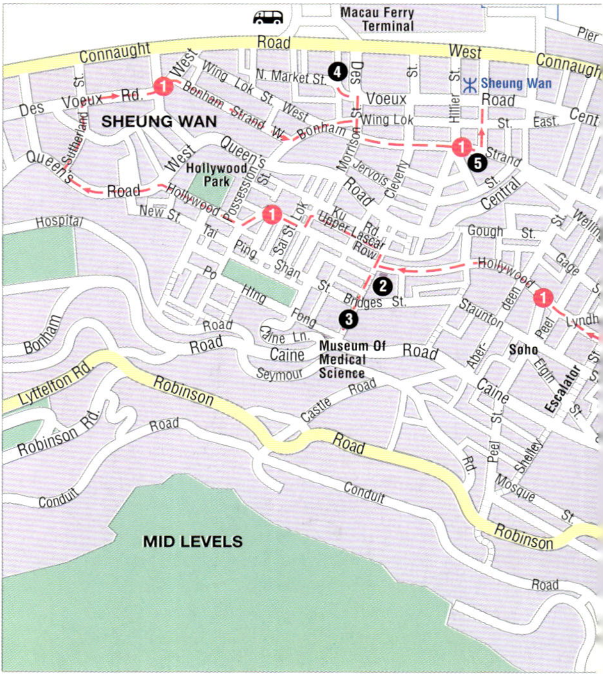

Back on Hollywood Road, there are still more shops. Beyond a bend in the road, **Possession Street** leads down to the right. It is hard to imagine now, but this used to be the waterfront, and Possession Street marks the spot where a decisive chapter of Hong Kong's history was written. Captain Charles Elliot landed in January 1841 and took possession of the island in the name of the British crown – somewhat over-hastily, as it turned out, because Her Majesty's Government would have preferred an island off the coast of Shanghai. Anyway, more than a year was to pass before the island was finally ceded following a few threatening gestures by the British warships off Nanking, which was the Chinese capital at the time. Elliot was summoned back to England because of his excessive zeal, instead of becoming the first governor. That honour was reserved for Sir Henry Pottinger.

A few yards further on is **Hollywood Park**, a modern interpretation of the traditional Chinese city garden. Old sepia photos on the notice board show how the area looked a century ago.

Soon after this the route arrives at **Queen's Road West**, another shopping street where household goods are offered alongside Chinese foodstuffs, especially rice of varying qualities in huge sacks. The visitor will be struck by the paper models of houses, cars, aircraft, furniture, etc. Fake paper money with an astronomically high face value, made out by the Bank of the Underworld, is stacked high in the shops. The items in question are not toys but gifts to be ceremonially burned on the grave of the deceased so that the dead can enjoy the 'good life' in the 'great beyond'. Come January, the shops are flush with red objects – red calendars, red motto-bearing ribbons, gift boxes and small bags – as the colour is considered lucky. At Chinese New Year, families redecorate their homes and distribute presents. The most popular presents are *lai see*, little red envelopes containing 'lucky' money.

Turn right into Sutherland Street. At the end of the road and in the wider expanse of Des Voeux Road West, which

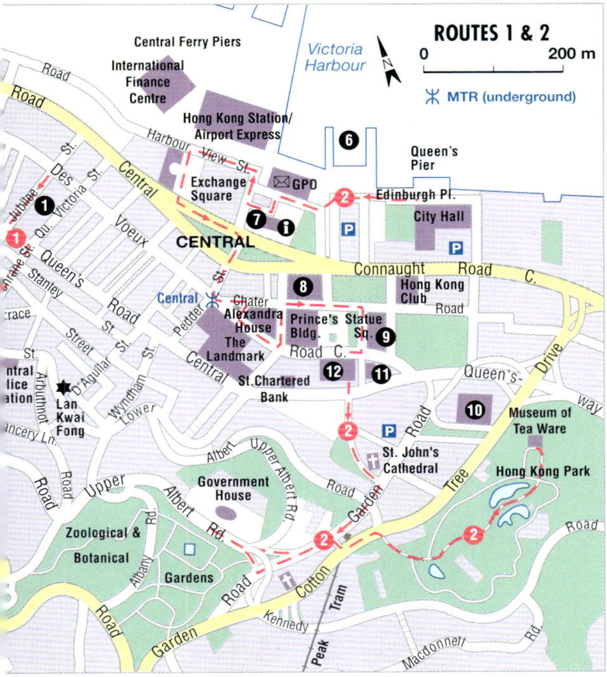

Hollywood Park

Herbal tea for sale

Chinese greens

can be distinguished by the tram lines which pass along it, there are countless shops offering dried foodstuffs, including mushrooms, shellfish and shrimps, as well as fruit, lotus nuts, sunflower seeds, pine kernels, biscuits and sweets. The mushrooms taste especially good; they simply need to be soaked in boiling water for a few minutes to make them tender and tasty once more.

In this district, streets named after the various governors adjoin one another. Sir Samuel Bonham (1848–54) leads off directly from Sir William Des Voeux (1887–91); to be more precise, the street is known as Bonham Strand West. Here are more shops selling dried foods, many alien to Western cuisine but considered by the Chinese to be gourmet delicacies. Bonham Strand West is the headquarters of the firms which import abalone, shark's fins, swallow's nests and ginseng. Ginseng is a root which grows primarily in Korea, in very finely sieved, humus-rich soil and which is dug up after several years. It is claimed that ginseng possesses healing as well as aphrodisiac properties; the latter is also claimed of abalone and shark's fin. Swallow's nests, cemented by the saliva of swallows, are harvested in Thailand and Vietnam by daring young men who retrieve the nests from cliffs when the young birds have hatched. In Bonham Strand West it is also possible to catch a glimpse inside the workshops where these foodstuffs are sorted, cut and packed.

Turning left, the route passes metalworkers' shops before arriving at a modern multi-storey food market. Many of the people working here previously had stalls in the colonial building of ★ **Western Market** ❹. The latter can be reached by following a narrow road on the left-hand side. It is a red brick building with beige decorative brickwork. Built in 1906, it is a fine example of Edwardian architecture. Fortunately, when it became too small and unhygienic, it was not torn down as were most other buildings dating from this period, but was sensitively restored and re-opened in 1991 as a period shopping mall. The fabric merchants upstairs relocated when the Cloth Alley bazaar was demolished, and their prices are fair. If you're thirsty, take a break in the Six Bugs Antiques & Café on the ground floor. The building's most attractive facade is on Connaught Road and is best viewed from the pedestrian overpass leading to the Macau Ferry Terminal.

Chop carver

The entire district is full of quaint and practical shops to interest the visitor. To put the seal of approval on this encounter with Chinese everyday life, visit one of the ★ **chop carvers** ❺. These chops, or seals, with engraved characters are thought to have been in use in China for some 3,000 years. They serve as signatures at the end of letters and contracts and also indicate ownership. Thus, pictures were signed not only by the artist on completion, but also by the purchaser. Prosperous Chinese officials would often possess a variety of seals charting their personal progress and development. Scholars laid great store by attractive and valuable seals. In former times, bronze, ivory, jade, amber, horn or crystallised stones were used. Today, the most common materials are clay, porcelain, bamboo, soapstone or plastic, the best material being a reddish stone known as 'Chicken's Blood'.

Most of the chop carvers are located on **Man Wa Lane**, a narrow alley running between Wing Lok Street (near the Sheung Wan MTR exit) and Bonham Strand (beside the HSBC branch). After surveying the goods on offer, choose a stone, a script type, and the way in which your name should be written. Latin script is no problem; if Chinese characters are preferred, the carver will have to transcribe your name phonetically by means of appropriate symbols. However, a true Chinese name also has a meaning which is closely linked to the character of its owner. Only a Chinese acquaintance who knows something about you will be able to give you such a name. In this case, ask the person to write it down for the chop carver. The oldest Chinese characters, traditionally used on seals, were introduced during the reign of the first emperor of the unified kingdom (221–206BC), Qin Shi Huangdi. The various strokes are grouped into rectangles with rounded corners to form the so-called official script. Many chop carvers are no longer fluent in this script, and so the newer everyday characters are also used.

Shops for browsing

Chops generally take from one to four hours to make, although complicated commissions may take longer. It is usual to make a down payment. Some carvers can also produce business cards on small hand printing presses.

If you are hungry after all that walking, there are plenty of good eating places in this part of town.

Route 2

Hong Kong Island: Central *See map pages 18–19*

When the British settled in their new colony, they called the capital Victoria, after their queen, who nearly rejected the island to which her foreign secretary, Lord Palmerston, disparagingly referred as a 'barren island'. Today, the built-up area extends right along the north coast, and its heart is prosaically known as Central or Central District. This is the financial and business hub, where land prices and rents are highest, which explains why the office blocks soar ever higher towards the sky. The shopping centres and boutiques bear most of the famous names from the international world of fashion. The headquarters of Hong Kong's principal banks mark the architectural highlights of the city. And only a couple of hundred yards beyond the towering skyscrapers you can relax in Hong Kong Zoological and Botanical Gardens or Hong Kong Park. To stroll past the shop windows and architectural sights a visitor should allow 2 to 3 hours.

Star Ferry and deck-hand

The route begins by the **Star Ferry Pier** ❻ from where the photogenic green and white ferries have been steaming across the harbour since 1898. A ★ **Star Ferry ride** at night is a highlight of any stay in Hong Kong. Directly adjacent lies the **Queen's Pier**, the government's official landing stage where private boats may also moor to take on passengers. Opposite, **City Hall**, a utilitarian 1962 building, houses a library, marriage registry, various city administration offices and one of Hong Kong's major cultural entertainment venues. Events information and tickets are available in the lobby. The attractive inner courtyard is decorated with trees and sculptures, which makes it a popular place for newly wed couples fresh from the Registry Office to pause for their first photos.

Leaving the City Hall, the slim high-rise to the east is still called the Prince of Wales Building, although its original tenants, the British armed forces, handed it over to the People's Liberation Army (PLA) in 1997.

The city's last remaining rickshaw drivers assemble on the covered exit path from the Star Ferry. They are delighted to pose for a photo – but strictly in exchange for dollars. Around the corner is the **General Post Office**, which offers temporary exhibitions of historic and commemorative stamps and a card shop, as well as the usual postal services. The tower just across the road is the 50-storey **Jardine House** ❼, whose 1,748 round windows have inspired the Chinese to nickname it the 'House of a Thousand Orifices'. Jardines is one of the oldest trading houses in the city; its colourful history provided much

Rush hour in the rain

of the inspiration for James Clavell's famous novels about Hong Kong: *Tai Pan* and *Noble House*. The HKTA Visitor Information Centre (Monday to Friday 9am to 6pm; Saturday 9am to 5pm; closed Sunday and public holidays) in the basement dispenses handy pamphlets, maps and events information.

To the west of the Star Ferry, the waterfront used to continue straight on. But now, together with the outlying islands' ferry piers, it has been moved further out into the harbour, all part of a massive land reclamation scheme to create more space for the Airport Express terminus, **Hong Kong Station** and International Finance Centre development. Behind it, the tinted glass and pink granite office complex of **Exchange Square** is home to the Hong Kong Stock Exchange (no visitors).

Reunion

Art galleries frequently use the lobby of the **Rotunda**, or upper lobby of One and Two Exchange Square, for exhibitions. A sculptural theme takes over in the podium courtyard area outside, which is decorated by fountains, two bronze ★ **Water Buffalo** by Dame Elizabeth Frink, a **Henry Moore** sculpture and a powerful statue of a ★ **Tai Chi Player** by Ju Ming. If you visit early in the morning, you may see the real thing as this is a favourite spot for tai chi practice. **Le Fauchon Café** to the side of the Tai Chi statue is a good place for refreshments and people watching.

The windows above the curved entrance to the rather squat Forum building represent stylised Chinese coins, which were round with square holes in the middle, through which they were threaded with string for safe keeping.

The underpass south of the Star Ferry Concourse leads to one of the world's top hotels, the **Mandarin Oriental** ❽. The Mandarin is also a Hong Kong social institution

Doorman at the Mandarin

Legislative Council Building

Statue Square

Bank of China

and its lobby lounge, restaurants and bars are popular rendezvous points for local residents to socialise with business acquaintances and friends.

At lunchtime, however, offfice workers are just as likely to be seen with a sandwich in their hand on **Statue Square** next door. On Sunday, the square and surrounding streets are chock-a-block with people, particularly Filipino domestic workers (or *amahs*) who gather here on their day off. In the north section of the square is a cenotaph commemorating the dead of two world wars. On the south side is a statue of Sir Thomas Jackson, an early chairman of Hongkong Bank.

The Hong Kong Club can be recognised by its narrow windows. The most powerful men in the city meet here. Their decisions have always been more far reaching than those made in the domed ★ **Legislative Council Building** (Legco) ❾, Hong Kong's equivalent of a parliament. The building previously housed the Supreme Court, the colony's final court of appeal. The foundation stone was laid in 1903, but construction was not completed until 1912. After the court moved to purpose-built law courts in Wanchai, the building underwent extensive interior alterations. In 1984, as the only colonial building remaining in the city centre, it was placed under a protection order. Sittings are held every Wednesday when Legco is in session (open to the public by prior reservation, tel: 2869 9399).

Across Queen's Road soars the Hong Kong headquarters of the ★★ **Bank of China** ❿. Its 1209-ft (369-m) tower is a landmark on the city skyline. The American-Chinese architect I.M. Pei demonstrated the power of Hong Kong's new rulers with this spectacular skyscraper. In 1982, the bank obtained the site from the Hong Kong government for a friendly 1.1 billion Hong Kong dollars, but financing problems and construction delays meant the bank was not ready for use until May 1990. The building attracted criticism from *feng shui* experts for its exterior form and general structure based on multiple triangles. Some say the angles direct bad *chi* towards the Legco Building.

Its predecessor, the old **Bank of China Building** ⓫, opposite Legco, seems almost modest in comparison. It is an attractive stone art deco-style building dating from 1950. The top floors, where the economic section of the Communist Party once met, today form an elegant rendezvous for Hong Kong's movers and shakers, who meet in the members-only China Club among choice Shanghai furnishings and an impressive collection of modern Chinese art.

The imposing building next door is the nerve centre of the venerable ★★ **Hongkong and Shanghai Banking Corporation (HSBC)** ⓬, known in the city by the understated abbreviation, 'The Bank'. Sir Norman Foster designed the building according to bridge-building principles and intentionally positioned technical facilities and services on the exterior, including those which are normally carefully hidden away. Completed in 1985, the building remains one of Hong Kong's most impressive landmarks. Even if you don't use their banking services it is worth taking the escalators up to the banking halls in order to appreciate the scale of the 170-ft (52-m) atrium.

The narrow reddish tower on the right is the headquarters of Hong Kong's third currency-issuing institution, the **Standard Chartered Bank**. From the 21st storey upwards, the floor area is reduced every six floors. In contrast to its major competitor the building's design is based on the octagon, which delighted the geomancers.

Passing beneath the Hongkong Bank, cross Queen's Road and climb the steps leading to the banyan-tree shaded **Battery Path**, past the elegant **Former French Mission Building** which houses the **Court of Final Appeal** (no visitors), and on to ★★ **St John's Cathedral**. Those who built what is thought to be the oldest Anglican church in East Asia (consecrated in 1849) could not decide between neo-Gothic and Norman styles, so settled on a mixture of the two, using local materials. During the Japanese occupation, the church was turned into a dance hall.

From St John's, you can walk up Garden Road to Upper Albert Road for a peek through the gates of **Government House**, home to 25 British governors from 1855 to 1997. It is now used to receive the Special Administrative Region's official guests (no visitors allowed). During World War II the Japanese commandant lived here and added the curious tower.

Lion on the Old Bank of China

'The Bank'

St John's stained-glass window

On the other side of Upper Albert Road lies another slice of colonial history, the **Hong Kong Zoological and Botanical Gardens** (daily 6am to 7pm). The British established botanical gardens in all their colonies to provide facilities for research into the local flora. This one was opened in 1864. The 600-odd plant species from tropical and subtropical habitats are clearly labelled. The gardens are a popular destination for family outings, and *tai chi chuan* is practised here by locals early every morning. The small zoo concentrating on primates and birds was added in 1975.

★★ **Hong Kong Park** (open daily 6.30am to 11pm) by contrast, is only a few years old. On the way the route passes the lower terminus of the **Peak Tram** (*see page 32*). The high-tech 32,300sq-ft (3,000sq-m) aviary houses magnificent brightly coloured birds from the Malaysian rainforest and other parts of Asia. Plant-lovers will head for the greenhouses, but the paths leading past the waterfalls also make an attractive walk. The park is a favourite spot for *tai chi* players to practise and wedding couples to pose for photos. If you're feeling energetic, you can climb the 105 steps of the 96-ft (30-m) observatory tower for a sweeping view of the park. Children are catered to with a 6-level playground; and a café and restaurant offer lunch and snacks.

The park site used to be known as Victoria Barracks, and ★ **Flagstaff House** (entered from Cotton Tree Drive) was the residence of the British military commander. This two-storey whitewashed house was completed in 1846 in the neo-Grecian manner and is one of Hong Kong's oldest surviving colonial buildings. Today, it houses the ★ **Museum of Tea Ware** (daily except Wednesday and public holidays 10am–5pm), in which centuries of tea culture are attractively presented.

Flagstaff House/ Museum of Tea Ware

Hong Kong Park fountain

Route 3

Hong Kong Island: Wanchai to Causeway Bay *See map pages 28–9*

Hong Kong's traditional means of public transport, the tram, also makes for an interesting alternative city sightseeing tour. After rattling along between the daily bustle of dark-suited businessmen in Central, housewives in Wanchai and shoppers in Causeway Bay, visitors can do their own shopping, relax in a park or visit a temple.

Introduced in 1904, Hong Kong's fleet of 160 ★ **electric trams** has remained virtually unchanged since the introduction of the familiar double-decker cars in 1925, apart from the addition of a horn which replaced the original bell in 1993. Redecorated annually according to advertising-agency whim, they run along the north coast of Hong Kong Island daily from 6am until 1am, or even all night on some public holidays. At HK$2 for adults, HK$1 for children, they offer what must be the cheapest city sightseeing tour in the world.

One of the famous trams

The main line heads away from Central along Queensway, through Johnston Road to Hennessy Road and then past Victoria Park to King's Road. A branch leads off through Percival Street to Happy Valley to the terminus south of the famous racecourse, making it an ideal starting point for visiting several interesting cemeteries.

In Central District the tram bumps past Statue Square, Legco Building and the headquarters of Hongkong Bank (HSBC), and the Bank of China. Next on the left is the many-sided mirrored facade of the **Lippo Centre**, formerly called the Bond Centre, after the later bankrupted Australian financial speculator Alan Bond, but now owned by an Indonesian industrial and banking group. Then come the Admiralty Centre and the United Centre, two mixed-use office and shopping complexes. Opposite is the building housing the city's Supreme Court, followed by a newer multi-functional shopping centre worthy of superlatives: **Pacific Place** ⑬. The lower levels are filled with shops, restaurants, Asian fast-food basements, wine bars and pubs as well as a cinema complex with four auditoriums for English-language films. Above lie 5½ million sq ft (½ million sq m) divided between offices and three hotels.

Lippo Centre and Pacific Place

The tram is now approaching **Wanchai**. To see a more traditional side of the district, you might want to disembark and make a detour up **Queen's Road East**, which marks Wanchai's original waterfront. Furniture shops offer rattan sofas, tables and chairs or traditional rosewood Chinese dining tables and chairs. The ★ **Hung Shing (Tai Wong) Temple** on the right has a boulder incorporated into its design and a sacred banyan tree behind. The circular **Hopewell Centre** was once the tallest building in Hong Kong. For a spectacular view, take the glass bubble lift between the 17th and 56th floors.

The ★ **Old Wanchai Post Office** (1912–13) was in operation until 1992. It now houses an Environmental Resource Centre (Monday to Saturday 10am to 5pm, Wednesday 10am to 1pm) and many of its original fittings have been preserved. Further on, **Stone Nullah Lane** to the right leads to an 1860s ★ **Pak Tai Temple** with a 10-ft (3-m) copper image of the Taoist god, made in 1604.

Devotees at Pak Tai

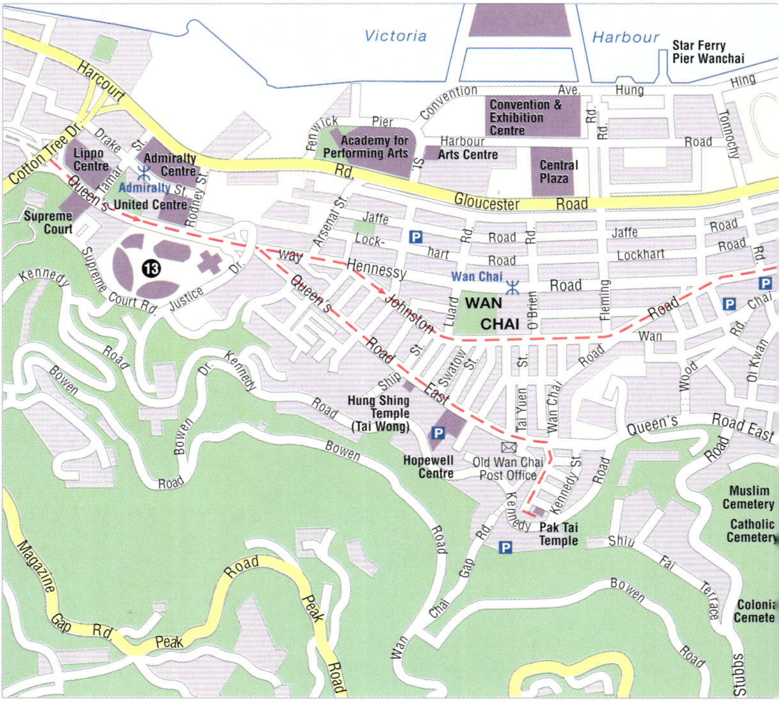

This side of Wanchai feels centuries apart from the gleaming modern structures that cluster on the reclaimed land along today's waterfront. Since 1985, the ★ **Hong Kong Academy For Performing Arts (APA)** has trained students in drama, music, dance and stage technique. Simon Kwan, the architect, accentuated the unusual ground plan with the frequent use of trianglese. Opposite lies the **Hong Kong Arts Centre** which includes a theatre, a cinema and galleries as well as the offices of cultural institutions. A little further east, sandwiched between the Grand Hyatt and Renaissance Harbour View hotels, is the ★ **Hong Kong Convention and Exhibition Centre**. Its low-rise extension jutting out into the harbour was completed in 1997, just in time to host the historic **Handover Ceremony** in which Britain formally returned Hong Kong to China at midnight on 30 June. Behind is Hong Kong's tallest building, **Central Plaza**, which at 1,227ft (374m) is the sixth highest in the world.

Back on the tram, the tracks fork right off Hennessy Road onto **Johnston Road**, another Wanchai street that has managed to retain some of its original character. Look out for a group of three narrow colonnaded 'shop-houses', once typical but now rare, and the traditional markets in the side streets on the right.

The tram rejoins Hennessy Road, the main thoroughfare between Wanchai and Causeway Bay. The typical combination of offices and shops continues along both sides of the street. Trams marked **Happy Valley** turn right along Percival Street, where shops selling electronics and stand cheek by jowl, before turning into Wong Nai Chung Road, wrapping around the race course to its Happy Valley terminus. Here you can either continue on foot or climb into the front tram and wait for it to move off again.

Happy Valley Race Course was established in the 1840s in a lush rice-growing valley unsuitable for settle-

A night at the races

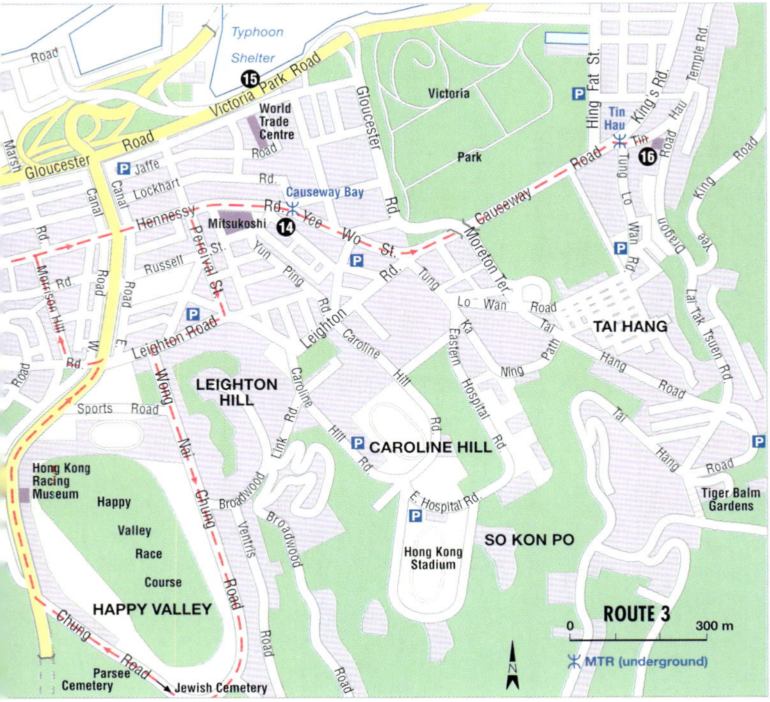

Jardine's Bazaar

ment due to malarial mosquitoes. Today, the track is surrounded by high-rises and has the state-of-the-art ★ **Hong Kong Racing Museum** (Tuesday to Sunday and some public holidays 10am to 5pm; Happy Valley race days 10am to 12.30pm) which traces the history of the sport. Wednesday ★ **evening race meetings** from September to June get packed with local residents, many of whom come for the gambling rather than the horses.

The ★ **Happy Valley cemeteries** (daily 8am to 6pm) on the other side of Wong Nai Chung Road provide further insight into Hong Kong's colonial history.

The Sikh temple

The lush green **Parsee Cemetery**, beside the Hindu temple to the south, is the most picturesque. The older headstones in the **Hong Kong ('Colonial') Cemetery** tell of early settlers' often premature deaths, while Portuguese memorials in **St Michael's Roman Catholic Cemetery** highlight the link with nearby Macau. There is a surprisingly high number of Chinese names in the **Muslim Cemetery**, from where you can look down onto the back of a 19th-century **Sikh Temple**. The memorials to many prominent Hong Kong citizens in the **Jewish Cemetery** are worth a detour up Shan Kwong Road. When you're ready, take a tram or walk back to Causeway Bay

Back on Hennessy Road, the route passes **Mitsukoshi**, one of several large Japanese department stalls which, along with the huge Times Square mall, contribute to the shopping mania of Causeway Bay. In **Jardine's Bazaar** and **Jardine's Crescent** ⓮, two smaller shopping streets, cheap clothing and fresh foods are for sale. The street names honour William Jardine, a trader who was one of the economic founders of the colony. With his partner, James Matheson, he established one of the most influential trading houses in Hong Kong. The company still plays an important role in the commercial life of the city.

The firm of Jardine Matheson also owns the ★ **Noonday Gun** ⓯, which is fired punctually every day. It stands by the Typhoon Shelter near the Excelsior Hotel. The safest way to cross the multi-lane carriageway is via the tunnel, accessible from the entrance to the World Trade Centre. The origins of the gun are somewhat obscure, although it is known that the opium traders had their own cannon and ammunition stores and were accustomed to greet their *Taipans* – the equivalent of today's senior board members – with a welcoming salvo as their ships entered harbour. However, the navy considered the privilege should be reserved for its senior officers and ordered Jardine Matheson to use up its remaining ammunition by firing a shot every day at noon. Until 1960, a 6-pounder rang out across the harbour, but people found it too loud, so Jardines halved the calibre.

The Noonday Gun

Passengers still on the tram will see **Victoria Park** on their left. The queen's monument is halfway along the street boundary. Locals use the park for *tai chi,* for walks and outings with the children. There are also football pitches as well as basketball, tennis and squash courts, a roller skating arena and a swimming pool. During the week before Chinese New Year a flower market is held here, attracting families well into the evening. The same is true of the Lantern Festival, when parents and children picnic on the grass with their elaborate lanterns.

Altar outside a home

Leave the tram just after the park and fork right up Tin Hau Temple Road. The ★ **Tin Hau Temple** ⓰ is perched on a granite ledge about hundred yards along. During the 18th century, when this area was still right on the waterfront, the inhabitants of the bay erected a temple in honour of the Taoist Queen of Heaven and patron goddess of fishermen and sailors. It is a simple building painted entirely in red, the colour of good fortune. Elderly women from the neighbourhood come to lay their offerings before the statue of Tin Hau on the central altar and to pay respect to their ancestors in the little room on the right. Numerous statuettes of Kwun Yum, the Buddhist Goddess of Mercy, have been placed in the little room on the left.

For a more flamboyant excursion into Taoist mysticism, take the No 11 bus from Leighton Road 17] to the ★ **Tiger Balm Gardens** (daily 9.30am to 4pm) on Tai Hang Road. Built in 1935 by the Singaporean millionaire philanthropist Aw Boon Haw, who made his fortune with Tiger Balm ointment, the gardens are filled with garish statues and bas-reliefs depicting scenes from Taoist hell. Now slightly worn around the edges but with a certain kitschy charm, the gardens have been under threat of redevelopment since early 1999, so it might be worth checking they're still open before you visit.

Route 4

Hong Kong Island: The Peak *See map page 32*

The world-famous ★★★ **panorama** from The Peak should be included in every visitor's itinerary. The journey to the top by the Peak Tram is an experience in itself, and from the observation pavilion or the viewing terrace at the Peak Tower visitors can gaze down on the jungle of skyscrapers and (on a clear day at least), the busy harbour and Kowloon peninsula over to the Nine Dragon Ridge, which separates metropolitan Hong Kong from the New Territories. At night the area becomes a dazzling spectacle of lights. A gentle stroll on the level path surrounding The Peak will take about an hour before dinner (you'll probably need insect repellent).

High above the harbour

The Peak, at 1,817ft (554m), the highest point on the island, was settled from the 1870s onwards on the advice of the chief medical officer of the colonial administration. The European residents wanted to escape from the densely built-up Western District and initially reserved the slopes facing the harbour for themselves. But transport up the steep slopes proved extremely tiresome, particularly as the Europeans were accustomed to being carried home in sedan chairs by coolies – a highly uncomfortable experience for all concerned in view of the uneven paths and steep incline.

And so it was not until the the ★★★ **Peak Tram** was constructed in 1888 that the Peak really came into its own and the era of the colonial villas on the airy heights was initiated. Until the completion of the Peak road in

1924, the tram remained the only public means of transport on the mountain. The Peak Tram is really a funicular railway and its two carriages are linked by a steel cable, so that the downhill tram partly helps to pull the other one in an uphill direction by its own weight. In 1926, the steam engine was replaced by an electric one, and since the renovation to mark the centenary of the tram, larger Swiss-built carriages with electronic controls, accommodating 120 passengers, have been in use.

The green No 1 minibus provides an alternative means of reaching the top. It leaves from Lung Wui Road to the east of City Hall in Central and scales the once inaccessible heights via Magazine Gap Road. The first road link was Stubbs Road, named after the governor of the time. The double-decker bus No 15 from Exchange Square also affords fine views of the city and the elegant villas. The residences of a number of consulates can be distinguished by the fluttering flags outside.

By whatever means the summit is reached, attention should be devoted firstly to the world-famous view of the city and harbour. Two good viewing spots are the terrace on Level 5 of the Peak Tower or the little observation pavilion to the east on narrow Findlay Road.

At this altitude there is usually at least a tepid breeze encouraging the visitor to make the circuit of the summit on foot. The narrow ★ **Lugard Road** starts directly opposite the **Peak Tower** tram terminus building, offering a fresh perspective at every bend. When the city disappears from sight, the islands of Lantau and Lamma appear on the horizon away to the west, whilst to the south the sun is reflected in the glittering South China Sea. The tree-lined path winding past isolated villas feels a world apart from the bustling metropolis below.

Lugard Road merges with Harlech Road at a junction and shady picnic spot. Continue east until the path brings you back to the start. From here, Mount Austin Road climbs steeply to the real summit, where there is a tropical park with magnificent views. There is no public transport to the top, but you can take a taxi from the Peak Tower.

Refreshments are next on the list and the Peak complex offers you several choices. Two of the pleasantest are the **Peak Café** (tel: 2849 7868), housed in what was originally a shelter for sedan chair bearers, and the **Café Deco** (tel: 2849 5111) in the Peak Galleria. It's a good idea to book ahead at weekends and holidays.

Other amusements on offer are the Ripley's Believe It or Not Odditorium and themed virtual reality rides in the Peak Tower; and souvenir shopping in the Peak Galleria (award-winning local designer Alan Chan's shop on Level 2 is a good place to start).

The new Peak Tram

The Peak Galleria

Aberdeen, harbour scene

Tin Hau temple

Route 5

Hong Kong Island: South Side *See map page 32*

While the north coast of Hong Kong is gradually being extended by the succession of land reclamation schemes, the south is characterised by long peninsulas, little bays with beaches, offshore islands and an almost resort-like atmosphere. Of course, there are high-rises here too, but the visitor will also discover numerous other gems. The complete tour of the south will take at least a day, but one can stop at any point and return to the city.

Buses No 7 and 71 run from Central through the Western District along the coast to Pokfulam and **Aberdeen** ⓱. Named after a British foreign secretary, Lord Aberdeen, in the 1840s, Aberdeen is one of the oldest settlements in Hong Kong. Indeed, its Chinese name, Heung Gong Tsai ('Little Fragrant Harbour') is thought to be the origin of the whole territory's name. This route begins in the old centre on Aberdeen Main Road. At the end of the road stands a little **Tin Hau** temple, built in 1851 by fishermen, although today one can hardly see the harbour from here. It is a simple temple with several inner courtyards linked together by round 'moon' gateways.

Follow Aberdeen Main Road down to the ★ **Aberdeen Harbour**. Although most descendants of Aberdeen's original Tanka and Hoklo 'boat people' now live in the surrounding high-rises, this is still one of Hong Kong's liveliest waterways. A sampan (small boat) ride here is a memorable highlight of any visit. The sampan operators (often surprisingly elderly women) keep an eye out for tourists and are always happy to negotiate a fee for a quick and occasionally rather hair-raising spin between the fishing trawlers, ramshackle live-aboard junks, upmarket yachts and pleasure craft, rounded off by three resplendently gaudy floating restaurants.

The Jumbo Floating Restaurant and sister establishments are an attraction in their own right, particularly when illuminated at night. Their free shuttle boats offer customers another chance to enjoy a trip through the harbour.

Lying on a narrow peninsula just south of Aberdeen is ★★ **Ocean Park** ⓘ, East Asia's largest entertainment complex (daily 10am to 6pm; adult admission HK$140; children HK$70). Highlights include the stunning **Atoll Reef and Shark Aquarium**; 360 degree views from the 236ft (72m) observation tower; cable car and escalator rides up and down the headland; the Raging River adventure ride. The **Middle Kingdom** section traces 5,000 years of Chinese history through cultural shows, artisan workshops and architectural reproductions. The most recent additions are two **giant pandas**, An An and Jia Jia, who reside in a HK$80 million air-conditioned habitat. To reach the park from Aberdeen, take a No 48 bus; the No 629 bus offers a direct service from the Star Ferry concourse in Central and Admiralty bus station.

Jumbo Floating Restaurant

Bus No 73 continues along the coast from Aberdeen (from Ocean Park's Wong Chuk Hang Road exit, you can take the southbound Nos 73, 6A or 260). The first port of call is **Deep Water Bay**, an address favoured by Hong Kong residents who can afford to build spacious villas on unobstructed slopes. Opposite the little beach lies the small but exclusive members-only HK Golf Course. In the bay, a flotilla of yachts rides at anchor; they belong to the Royal Hong Kong Yacht Club, which has one of its three clubhouses on Middle Island, just a few yards from the shore.

As the bus rounds the next headland, **Repulse Bay** comes into view, dominated by a massive wall of condominiums that made local headlines when it was built in 1982. In the middle of its gently curving facade is a large rectangular hole into which at least another 10 flats would have fitted. The story has it that the developers left the hole free for *feng shui* reasons (so the mountain's 'dragon spirit' still had access to the sea). The bus stops at the foot of the complex in front of **The Repulse Bay**, a colonial-style building which is a replica of the old Repulse Bay Hotel (1920), pulled down to make way for the condo development behind. The original had been a summer resort popular amongst the colonial administrators and visiting celebrities such as the writer Graham Greene.

In its present incarnation as an upmarket restaurant and shopping complex, it is home to two of Hong Kong's most romantic restaurants, the **Verandah** (European; tel: 2315 3166) and **Hei Fung Terrace** (dim sum and Cantonese; tel: 2812 2622).

Spyhole for a dragon

Repulse Bay beach

Jewellery in Stanley Market

Stanley's Tin Hau Temple

★ **Repulse Bay**, named after a 19th-century British warship involved in hunting local pirates, is the most famous bay in south Hong Kong. The beach has a wide range of amenities from changing rooms and showers to fast-food restaurants, which makes it a favourite weekend excursion for city-dwellers. One of its more curious attractions is the whimsical collection of Budhhist and Taoist statues that watch over the swimmers from the ★ **Life Guard Club** at the south end of the beach. The No 73 bus continues on to ★ **Stanley** ⓳. If you're re-boarding at Repulse Bay you can also take the No 6, 6A, 63, 65 and 260 buses on to this next destination.

Stanley, named after a British colonial minister, lies at the narrowest point on a long spit of land, the southern section of which is military property. It is therefore advisable to disembark at the end of Stanley Village Road, and join in the lively atmosphere of ★★ **Stanley Market** (daily 10am–6pm). Shoes and textiles are the most common items, although there are also typical Chinese souvenirs. The quality is mostly better than at the Temple Street Night Market, with correspondingly higher prices. Good buys include embroidered household linens, silk clothing, international brand name 'seconds' and sports shoes.

Continue through the market towards the exit on Stanley Main Street, which overlooks Stanley Bay. Beyond the strip of bars and restaurants is a tiny Tai Wong Temple built into a rock. Continue north to Stanley's ★ **Tin Hau Temple**, one of the oldest on Hong Kong island. Two stories revolve around the temple. Apparently, when the Japanese attacked Hong Kong during World War II, the villagers hiding in the temple saw a bomb fall onto the square in front. They ascribed the fact that it did not explode to the protective influence of the goddess.

The other story relates to the rather tatty tiger skin displayed inside, which was reputedly shot in front of the **Old Stanley Police Station** (now an upmarket restaurant) in 1942. The temple used to be on the seashore but recent reclamation has left it surrounded by a modern housing development. This is at least partially compensated by the reconstruction of **Murray House**, a colonial military barracks dating from 1843 which was knocked down in 1982 to make way for the Bank of China tower in Central. Its new incarnation as a complex of trendy bars and restaurants is scheduled to open in early 2000.

The quickest way back to Central for those who wish to end their exploration here is by bus No 6A, 6X or 260, which all take the tunnel route (for Tsim Sha Tsui and Kowloon, you can take the No 973). The journey on to Shek O is more complicated as there is no direct public transport link. The No 14 bus runs along Tai Tam Road above the village centre and on to Shau Kei Wan on the north coast of Hong Kong Island where one can then take the No 9 bus to Shek O or change to a minibus. It is also possible to change buses and take the No 9 at the roundabout where the Shek O Road branches off from Tai Tam Road. If all this sounds too complicated, the alternative is to take a taxi.

Tai Tam Road follows the coast and affords fine views of the sea. It is not surprising, therefore, to find that the hillside below the road is dotted with houses which are only accessible from above. Then two huge tower blocks appear, one of them named after Hong Kong's rival in skyscraper construction, Manhattan. The residents enjoy splendid views which compensate for the long journey into town. There is an interesting housing estate on the Red Hill Peninsula, with exclusive Spanish-style terraced houses built on different levels.

The next landmark is the narrow wall surrounding the Tai Tam Tuk reservoir. In fact there are three interlinked reservoirs in all, surrounded by a network of attractive country footpaths. The road then climbs uphill to reach the roundabout mentioned above, at which point one can change to the No 9 bus. The latter continues down the **D'Aguilar Peninsula**, named after the first commander-in-chief of the British military forces in the new colony. Most of the peninsula is taken up by the ★ **Shek O Country Park**, which is crossed by a number of hiking routes, including the famous ★ **Dragon's Back ridge walk**. The ridge runs at an average 600 ft (200m) in height, but the park's peaks reach 1,500 ft (347m), 1,000 ft (325m) and 900 ft (284m). There is usually a fresh breeze up on the top of the mountains as well as magnificent views of the sea on both sides. Walkers shouldn't forget drinking water and suntan lotion, as there are no shade-giving trees.

Shek O is a curious village in which some families have lived for decades in modest village houses next to the magnificent villas of wealthy neighbours. The postman's job is particularly difficult as the house numbers appear to be re-allotted at random every year. It is pleasant to stroll through the village streets to its little central square, where there is an attractive temple.

During the week, the beach is one of the quietest and most attractive on the island. There is a popular Thai-Chinese restaurant called the **Shek O Chinese-Thai Seafood** (open daily 11am to 10pm) by the roundabout at the entrance to the village. For a mellow café restaurant atmosphere, try the **Black Sheep** (Tuesday to Saturday 5pm to midnight).

Getting back to town is not quite so complicated. The No 9 bus and minibuses run to Shau Kei Wan, from where the MTR provides a rapid return to the centre.

Stanley local

Shek O beach

Tsim Sha Tsui ferry terminal

A cruise ship approaches

The Clock Tower

Route 6

Kowloon *See map pages 40–1*

Nathan Road seems to exert a magical attraction on the shoppers of this world. Every day, thousands of them throng in front of its shop windows before haggling over prices inside. But Tsim Sha Tsui, the tip of Kowloon Peninsula, is also the home of Hong Kong's major museums and cultural entertainment venue. Further up the peninsula, life remains more traditional and down-to-earth. Markets selling everything one can possibly imagine dominate the scene until the evening, when the Temple Street Night Market gets into full swing. To do the sights on this tour justice, you'll need a full day. However, their proximity to public transport means you can pick and mix according to your preference and the time available.

Take note of the time by the **Clock Tower** ⓴ – the only remains of the original Kowloon-Canton Railway terminus – directly next to the Star Ferry Pier. Don't insist on accuracy though, for the four clocks on the faces of the tower are not synchronised and therefore do not always show the same time. In 1975, the railway station was torn down and replaced by a modern building in Hung Hom but the clock tower (built in 1916) was renovated and preserved. Where the tracks used to be, palm trees now frame a succession of interlinked pools. The large bronze sculpture of the *Flying Frenchman* was created by the French artist Cesar Baldaccini (1921–98).

On the site of the former railway station, the tiled façade of the **Hong Kong Cultural Centre** rises skywards. Officially opened in 1989, the centre houses two large concert halls and a studio theatre, all frequently used by the Hong Kong Philharmonic Orchestra and visiting performers. However, it is difficult to understand why the government, despite its determination to create a cultural centre of international standing, granted planning permission for the architect José Lee's almost windowless building on a site which enjoys one of the most magnificent views in the world.

Visitors can enjoy the view across to Hong Kong Island, however, by taking a stroll along the **Waterfront Promenade** – something which should be done at least twice during any stay, once by day and once by night. The tips of the skyscrapers reaching up out of the modernistic jungle on the other side of the harbour soar ever higher, and with a bit of luck, a freighter will sail across the scene, framing the view for photography.

A break from shopping

The ★ **Hong Kong Museum of Art** ㉑ (Monday to Wednesday and Friday to Saturday 10am–6pm; Sundays and public holidays 1–6pm) stands directly on the waterfront. Exhibited in various galleries are pictures portraying Hong Kong as well as old Chinese works, a valuable collection of Chinese paintings and calligraphy and the classics of the contemporary Hong Kong School. Since the beginning of this century, this group of artists have been searching for a synthesis of East and West, although for many years they were 'too Chinese' for the West and too modern for the Orient. Today, the reputation of their works as 'classics' is denied by no one.

The first museum in the cultural complex was established in 1980 on Salisbury Road. The egg-shaped ★ **Space Museum** ㉒ (Monday and Wednesday to Friday 1–9pm, Saturday, Sunday and public holidays 10am–9pm; children under 3 years not admitted) is dedicated to the conquest of space and the exploration of the stars. Its high-tech Space Theatre planetarium features wide-screen Omnimax films and Sky shows several times daily.

Space Museum

On the other side of Salisbury Road stands the grand dame of Hong Kong hotels, **The Peninsula**. Opened on 11 December 1928, it was the first hotel on Kowloon, strategically positioned for passengers travelling overland to Europe by train. The ★★ **Peninsula Lobby** became the favourite rendezvous for high society: to this day, guests sit beneath the gilt stucco and potted palms to see and be seen. Tea or evening cocktails to strains of the resident string orchestra are a wonderful way to recapture the atmosphere of a bygone age (dress code has been relaxed until 6.30pm, but shorts and men's sandals are never welcome). Modernists might prefer the Philippe Starck-designed **Felix** restaurant-cum-bar and nightclub in the 30-storey extension tower.

Exit via the Peninsula Shopping Arcade onto bustling **Nathan Road**, which is lined with shops, hotels, restau-

The modern mosque

Tai Chi in Kowloon Park

rants and has been dubbed **Kowloon's 'Golden Mile'**. Its early 20th-century nickname was 'Nathan's Folly', poking fun at the governor, Matthew Nathan, for building a wide tree-lined avenue on the almost unpopulated Kowloon peninsula when the colony's social life centred almost exclusively on Hong Kong Island.

Just past the junction of Haiphong Road, on the left, is the modern **Kowloon Mosque**. This is the largest mosque in Hong Kong and the spiritual abode of 50,000 Muslims. It stands on the site of a late 19th-century mosque built for Muslim troops stationed in the British army barracks at what is now **Kowloon Park** (daily 6am to midnight). Inside the park, a few yards on the right, is a path leading to the sculpture garden where artists from Hong Kong and further afield display their work. Behind is the maze from where paths lead to the flamingo pool, children's playgrounds, pavilions and the formal gardens.

From Kowloon Park, choose one of two options. The first is to cross Nathan Road and walk east along **Granville Road**, famous for its 'factory outlet' shops selling 'seconds' or over-runs of garments manufactured locally for export. You can pick up some great bargains here. At the end of the street, take the raised pedestrian walkway over

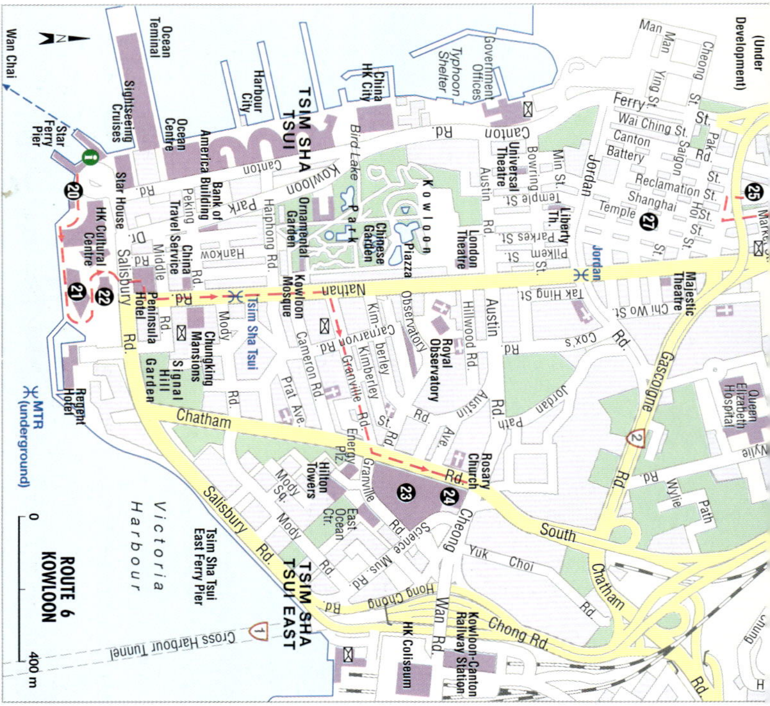

Chatham Road South. Follow the signs to the ★ **Hong Kong Science Museum** ㉓ (Tuesday to Friday 1pm to 9pm; weekends and some public holidays 10am to 9pm; closed Monday and some public holidays) a wonderland of interactive, hands-on exhibits exploring the mysteries of science and technology.

Next door at No 100 is the ★ **Hong Kong Museum of History** ㉔ (Monday to Thursday, Saturday 10am to 8pm; Sunday and holidays 1pm to 8pm; closed Friday). The museum has recently relocated and its permanent exhibition is scheduled to open in Autumn 2000. This will trace the evolution of Hong Kong over 6,000 years, from a peaceful rural backwater to a teeming metropolis. In the interim, the Special Exhibition Gallery will host exhibitions of historical photographs and other related topics.

The second option on the tour takes in ★ **Kowloon's street markets**. The nearest of these is the ★ **Jade Market** ㉕ (daily 10am to 3.30pm) on Kansu Street beneath the elevated road. Untreated and polished stones as well as finished items of jewellery are displayed in widely varying qualities. You are more likely to find an attractive souvenir than a valuable heirloom. Jade has a long history as a

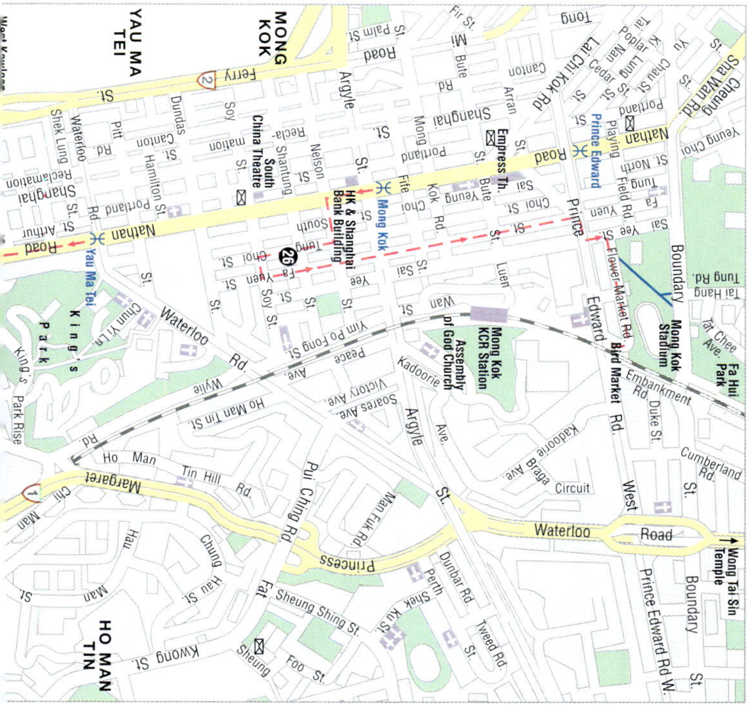

Jade Market jewellery

Browsing for bargains

decorative stone in Chinese culture. It is usually green, occasionally white, and attracts extremely high prices throughout East Asia. Huge pieces weighing several tons can be seen adorned with delicate carvings of landscapes in temples and palaces. In Hong Kong, the superstitious use jade amulets to ward off evil spirits.

The best route to the Jade Market is from Yau Ma Tei MTR station (Man Ming Lane, exit C), turning right down Nathan Road and right again onto Public Square Street. This takes you past a little park and a quartet of temples named after the most famous of the four, the ★ **Tin Hau Temple**. Tin Hau, the patron goddess of fishermen and sailors, was the daughter of a fisherman who lived in Fujian Province on the coast of mainland China in the 13th century. After she miraculously survived a tempest, Kublai Khan, the Mongol emperor, nominated her Tin Hau, or 'Queen of Heaven'. In the Taoist pantheon she ranks second only to the Jade Emperor. Her temple stands opposite the park entrance, with her statue against the far wall.

To the left of the Tin Hau Temple is a shrine to the city deity, Shing Wong. He ensures justice and law on earth and in the underworld and is thus accompanied by judges and soldiers. Further to the left, in the Fok Tak Temple, are a number of different deities, bearing witness to a strong element of religious tolerance as well as to a certain arbitrariness in the selection of gods.

To the right of the Tin Hau Temple, local gods are revered in the Shea Tan Temple, but the visitor will also re-encounter statues of Kwun Yum, Wong Tai Sin, Man, the God of Literature, and Mo, the God of War. Simple stones demonstrate that animist traditions are still very much alive.

The route continues through the neighbouring streets where the shops have been modernised, but where traditional wares are still on sale: temple goods such as statues of deities, candlesticks, incense sticks and sandalwood, and household items for the Chinese kitchen from woks and huge ladles to choppers and chopping boards. Shanghai Street is full of shops which specialise in wedding attire. In former times, Chinese brides wore red – the colour of good fortune. The white worn by brides in the West, which is the Christian symbol of purity, symbolises mourning in China. Today the displays along Shanghai Street are geared to both traditions.

At varying times of day, food markets are set up along some of the streets in the neighbourhood, although their existence is threatened by the rapid changes taking place in the area. From Yau Ma Tei, one stop north on the MTR brings you to Mong Kok station. After taking the Nelson Street exit, continue past the first two intersections as far as Tung Choi Street. This is the scene of the busy

Happy Buddha

Fish for supper

★ **Ladies' Market** ❷⓺ (noon to 10.30pm). A variety of clothing and shoes, household goods, jewellery and watches are displayed on the stalls.

Continue north on Tung Choi Street, crossing busy Argyle Street and Mong Kok Road. This end of Tung Choi Street, known as **Goldfish Market** (10am to 6pm), is where Hong Kong people buy the fish and aquariums considered lucky in *feng shui*. The parallel section of **Fa Yuen Street** is known for its factory outlet shops and is a good place to pick up genuine fashion bargains.

At the north end of Fa Yuen Street, cross busy Prince Edward Road West, head one block east, take the first left into Sai Yee Street and first right into fragrant Flower Market Road, home to Hong Kong's premier ★ **Flower Market** (10am to 6pm). At the far end you will find the ★**Yuen Po Street Bird Garden** (7am to 8pm).

For centuries, songbirds have been the most popular pets in Chinese households. Their owners take them for walks every day, carrying the cloth-covered cages through the streets and only removing the covers when they are hung up on trees in the park. Here, the birds entertain passers-by with a symphony of shrill arias. As well as birds, you will find intricately-made cages for sale, and a selection of porcelain containers for food and water. There's also a lively trade in crickets, which are also kept by the Chinese as domestic musicians.

Kowloon's most famous market, ★★ **Temple Street Night Market** ❷⓻ (best between 7pm and 10pm) runs three blocks west of Jordan MTR station (exit A). Fabrics, leather goods, fake watches, electronic gadgets, CDs and videos – mostly cheap-label versions – are the main items on offer. Although everything is remarkably cheap, bartering is an intrinsic part of the shopping experience.

Songbirds are popular pets in Hong Kong

Temple Street Night Market

Route 7

The Eastern New Territories *See backcover map*

Where rice seedlings once sprouted in muddy paddy fields in the New Territories, concrete towers and housing blocks now rise skywards. Visitors can combine their impressions of everyday life in suburban Hong Kong with a visit to a number of interesting temples. The KCR overland railway provides rapid transportation out of town, so a trip to the Eastern New Territories will take a whole day.

The first stop should be at Hong Kong's most active, significant and wealthy temple. The ★★ **Wong Tai Sin Temple** (daily 7am to 5.30pm; small donation expected) is signposted and easy to get to from Wong Tai Sin MTR station (exit B2).

According to legend, Wong Tai Sin was a shepherd boy in the Chinese province of Zhejiang. At the age of 15, an immortal taught him the art of transforming vermilion into a medicine which could heal all diseases. Wong Tai Sin was regarded as a miracle worker, but as he could also foretell the future he was revered as a demi-god after his death. Hong Kong residents visit his temple not only to beg for healing for themselves or someone else, and to ask for help with business problems, but also to have their futures prophesied. Within the temple compound is a large chemist's shop and numerous booths for fortune tellers who interpret the arcane texts which the faithful receive inside the temple. It is one of the largest concentrations of fortune tellers in Asia.

Immigrants brought the first statue of Wong Tai Sin to Hong Kong in 1915 and placed it in a small temple in Wanchai. In 1921, his followers founded a charitable

Worshippers at Wong Tai Sin

organisation known as Sik Sik Yuen, which moved the temple from crowded Wanchai to the then sparsely inhabited Kowloon. The 1920s building was demolished in 1968 and replaced by this impressive new complex which has been open to the public since 1973. The temple is at its most lively and crowded during the Chinese New Year festival and on the 23rd day of the eighth lunar month, which is the festival of Wong Tai Sin.

The courtyard in front of the main temple – which is Buddhist, Taoist and Confucian – is on the left behind the imposing entrance door. Most of the worshippers in the courtyard are women, who spend the entire day making sacrifices to Wong Tai Sin or shaking the bamboo spills for the fortune tellers. The picture of the Taoist deity can only be glimpsed at the far end of the ornate hall, which is almost always too crowded to cross.

On the right near the main hall stands the considerably smaller temple of the Three Saints. These are Kwun Yum, the Goddess of Mercy, in the middle, Kwan Ti, the God of War on the right, and Lü Dong Bin, one of the eight Taoist Immortals, on the left. In a neighbouring hall, the ancestral tablets of the deceased members of the Sik Sik Yuen are preserved. The next building is dedicated to Confucius and 72 of his most important disciples. The big hall on the far right is used for meetings and celebrations, and the building in front contains offices and a library. On the way back to the entrance you will pass the Yue Heung shrine to the Buddha of Light on the right, and a chemist's shop on the left.

Behind the temple and separate from it, lies the temple garden (daily 7am–5.30pm), which can only be reached through a single entrance. A particular attraction amongst the rocks, shrubs, streams and waterfalls is the Long Walk from the Summer Palace and the Nine Dragons Wall from the Imperial Palace in Beijing, which were copied here on a smaller scale.

In order to reach the New Territories proper by MTR, it is necessary to travel two stations back in the direction of Yau Ma Tei in order to change at Kowloon Tong to the KCR. The train reaches hilly country after a few minutes and passengers may catch a glimpse of two famous rock formations on the right-hand side. The **Lion Rock** is shaped like a lion's head, but the **Amah (Mother) Rock** owes its name to a legend. A fisherman's wife waited for so long for her husband to return after a storm that she was turned to stone, along with the child strapped to her back. The Chinese are known for their imaginative interpretation of natural forms.

Two stations after Kowloon Tong, the train reaches Sha Tin, one of the New Towns which have grown up in the

Offerings and other items

Ten Thousand Buddhas Monastery

Po Fook Ancestral Hall

Praying in the temple

New Territories since the 1970s and which continues to expand today. Although half the population already lives in government-sponsored housing, the constant migration to the metropolis means that the demand is as great as ever, and that living conditions continue to be very cramped. The shopping centre and the residential area of Sha Tin begin on the far side of the station. If time allows, plunge into the masses to see for yourself.

The main reason for stopping at Sha Tin is to visit the ★★ **Man Fat Tze** or **Monastery of Ten Thousand Buddhas** (daily 9am to 5pm) which is set up 400 steps (there's an escalator for those in a rush or not up to the climb) and well-signposted from Sha Tin KCR station. On the way is the **Po Fook Ancestral Hall**, opened in 1990. Thousands of urns containing the ashes of the dead are preserved in this Tang Dynasty-style mausoleum. In front of the fence marking the limits of the complex is a narrow footpath leading to the steps which good Buddhists climb to reach the temple, thereby gaining merit for rebirth. The Monastery of Ten Thousand Buddhas was founded in 1957 by the monk Yuet Kai who died in 1965 at the age of 87. He had previously predicted that his body would not decompose if he were to be buried behind the temple in a crouching position. True enough, when his disciples exhumed the body eight months later, they found it still in good condition. They covered his corpse in gold leaf and placed it in a building on the second level.

The main prayer hall lies on the first level. The large Buddha statues on the main altar, together with Kwun Yum, a healing goddess and the Ruler of Heaven and Earth, are surrounded by 12,800 smaller Buddha statues, all donated, positioned in the niches around the walls. Very conspicuous are the brightly coloured concrete and plaster figures in the forecourt, which gleam in all the colours of the rainbow. The figures on each side represent the 18 *Luohan*, the most important disciples of the Buddha; in the central pavilion is a Fasting Buddha as well as the animal companions of wise men in Chinese mystic writings. The forecourt provides a fine view over Sha Tin and the surrounding countryside.

A branch line of the KCR which only operates on racing days leads to the modern ★ **Sha Tin Race Course**, worth the detour only if a race is on. Up to 85,000 spectators can follow the races through binoculars or with the aid of the huge video wall. The most important aspect, of course, is the betting, which here is fully computerised. People also come here to enjoy the **Penfold Park** bird sanctuary in the centre of the track (closed race days and Monday, except public holidays).

Get off at the next KCR station, University, and take the shuttle bus to the ★ **Chinese University Art Gallery** (Monday to Saturday 10am–4.45pm, Sunday 12.30–5.30pm, closed some public holidays), which has a fine collection of paintings and calligraphy from Guangdong Province, 300 bronze seals from the Han-Dynasty period and earlier, and over 400 jade carvings.

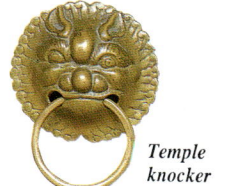
Temple knocker

Race meeting at Sha Tin

Disembark at **Tai Po Market** station and take a taxi to the ★ **Man Mo Temple** in Fu Shin Street. Like its namesake in Hollywood Road, the temple is dedicated to the God of Literature, Man, and the God of War, Mo. The inscriptions at the entrance of the temple, founded in 1892, indicate the individual roles of the deities: 'The God of Literature controls the sun and the moon' and 'The God of War controls the mountains and rivers'. On the main altar, Man holds a paintbrush and a sceptre; Mo, who has a red face, holds a sword. Above the doors of the main hall on both sides of the inner courtyard are representations of bats. In China, bats are considered to be symbols of good luck, because the Chinese words for 'Good Luck' and 'Bat' sound very similar.

In the street in front of the temple, a **market** is set up daily, continuing a former village tradition. The people who originally lived here were mostly Tanka, who made a good living as pearl collectors in Tolo Harbour. During the 17th century the village was well known for its market, which served a wide surrounding area.

Fu Road, at the bottom of the street, leads round to the ★ **Hong Kong Railway Museum** (9am to 5pm; closed Tuesday and some public holidays) at 13 Shun Tak Street. The picturesque building, which looks more like a temple than a station, was the original Tai Po Market Station (1913). There is an old-fashioned booking office with displays of memorabilia inside, and carriages of different periods stand outside the museum.

Hong Kong Railway Museum

Tsing Ma Bridge

Lei Cheng Uk

Route 8

The Western New Territories

Central Hong Kong prides itself on its modernity. Until a few years ago, even early colonial buildings were torn down without a second thought. But a wind of change is blowing through the skyscrapers. In the New Territories, with the assistance of village residents, ambitious restoration schemes are being undertaken to preserve the remains of the old Chinese inheritance in the region: ancestral halls, walled villages and temples. In view of the somewhat complicated transport connections, an entire day should be set aside for the described route.

The fact that Hong Kong was settled way back in the days of the Han Dynasty some 2,000 years ago is proved by the existence of the ★ **Lei Cheng Uk Han Tomb** (Monday to Wednesday, Friday and Saturday 10am to 1pm and 2pm to 6pm; Sunday and some public holidays 1pm to 6pm). The tomb was discovered during construction work in the Sham Shui Po district of Kowloon in 1955, and named after its location in the village of the families Lei and Cheng. The cross-shaped vault is made of bricks and was built without the use of mortar. Inside the grave, 58 tiny funeral offerings were found, copies of everyday objects which were intended to accompany the deceased beyond the grave. But neither body nor skeletal remains were found, and experts were unable to decide upon the exact significance of the grave.

Today, visitors can peer into the vault and study the grave offerings exhibited in the on-site museum. The tomb is located in the middle of a public housing estate at 41 Tonkin Street, four blocks north of the Cheung Sha Wan MTR station.

Continue by MTR to Tsuen Wan Station (Exit B). From here you have a choice of activities. If you'd like to learn more about Hong Kong International Airport, take a No 96M maxicab to Ting Kau to see the ★ **Airport Core Programme Exhibition Centre** (Tuesday to Friday 10am to 5pm; weekends and some holidays 10am to 6.30pm). As well as airport-related exhibits, the centre offers good views of the ★ **Tsing Ma Bridge**, at 1.40 miles (2.2km), the world's longest road-and-rail suspension bridge.

If you're more interested in tradition than modern transport, follow the signs from Exit B to the ★★ **Sam Tung Uk Museum** (Wednesday to Monday 9am to 5pm; closed Tuesday and some public holidays) on Kwu Uk Lane. This small walled village, whose Cantonese name translates as 'Three-beamed dwelling', was founded by the Chans, a Hakka family, in 1786. Today, dwarfed by high-rise housing estates, it displays period furniture and farming implements, and exhibitions on Chinese folk culture. Another traditional Hakka dwelling, the **Hoi Pa Village Old House**, survives as an Environmental Resource Centre in a little park off Tsuen Wan Market Street.

Sam Tung Uk Museum

The next stage in this journey into Hong Kong's past will be by bus, the No 66M to Tai Hing housing estate in Tuen Mun from the bus terminus beneath the CRC Department Store (signed from Tsuen Wan MTR station exit A2). It crosses the motorway towards Tuen Mun. To the right of the road the vista is dominated by mountain scenery, while to the left there is a good view of the harbour and the **Tsing Ma Bridge**. Tuen Mun is one of the oldest settlements in the territory. During the Tang Dynasty era (618–907), a fortress guarded the entrance to the Pearl River. Later, it was expanded to create a naval base. From the 11th century, the Tang clan, which came from the province of Jiangxi, settled in the region and farmed the fertile hinterland. Today, Tuen Mun is another of the huge New Towns.

Get off the bus at its Tai Hing Estate terminus, turn right out of the terminus along Tai Fong Street and left onto the Tsun Wen Road. You can see the roof of your next destination, the ★★ **Ching Chung Koon Monastery** ahead, just beyond the highway bridge. Also known as the Temple of the Green Pine Trees, it was founded by a Taoist association in 1949 in honour of Lu Dong Bin, one of the eight immortals. The temple is principally known for its collection of some 4,000 books on Taoism and Chinese history, and for its more than 1,000 bonsai trees.

Figurine at Ching Chung Koon Monastery

Approaching through a huge ceremonial gateway, the visitor first arrives in front of a bell tower and a drum tower. In earlier times both instruments were used to indicate the time. Behind stands the main hall with a gilt statue of the immortal and two of his disciples. According to legend, Lü Dong Bin fell asleep while on his way to the capital in order to take the civil service entrance examination. In a dream he saw his future and decided, on waking up 18 years later, to live as a hermit.

Further to the left, ancestral tablets of the dead are preserved in this peaceful temple. A large part of the complex serves as a home for the aged run by the social organisation of the Taoist Association, which also serves visitors a vegetarian meal at midday.

Leave the monastery by the path to the left of the one by which you entered. You'll see the Ching Chung Light Rail Transit (LRT) stop ahead. Cross the tracks and take the No 615 towards Yuen Long. Look out for the ★ **Miu Fat Buddhist Monastery** across the busy Castle Peak Road on the right. Two powerful dragons guard the entrance to the Buddhist monastery. The hall of the temple is the largest in Southeast Asia; more than 10,000 Buddha statues and paintings representing episodes in the life of the Buddha in Chinese and Thai style adorn the walls. To visit, disembark at the Lam Tei stop. Otherwise, stay on the LRT as far as the Ping Shan stop.

Dragon Gateway, Miu Fat Monastery

Walk back a little from the station and then turn right into Ping Ha Road. After approximately 400yds (about 370m) you will reach the Hung Shing Temple, which is the starting point for the ★★ **Ping Shan Heritage Trail**. The footpath, about ½ mile (1 km) long, is clearly signposted and leads through the villages of Ping Shan past several small temples and ancestral halls of the Tang clan to Hong Kong's only remaining pagoda. Villagers allow visitors to look round most of the monuments on the trail between 9am and 5pm (except for Chinese New Year), but please respect the fact that they are private monuments.

The **Hung Shing Temple** is a simple building dating from the end of the 18th century, and dedicated to an exceptionally able Tang-dynasty official. He was skilled in astronomy and able to give the fishermen accurate weather forecasts, which is why they continued to honour him after his death.

Book in Kun Ting Study Hall

Nearby lies the **Kun Ting Study Hall** (closed to visitors in July 1999, but may shortly re-open). This hall was built in 1870 by a member of the Tang clan in memory of his father. Designed like a country villa, the building served as a school for the sons of the Tang family; those who came from other villages stayed in **Ching Shu Hin**

(which was also closed to visitors in July 1999), the neighbouring house.

Ping Shan Heritage Trail

On the edge of the village lies the main **Tang Ancestral Hall**. According to clan records, there has been a Tang family ancestral hall on this site for about 700 years. The **Yu Kiu Ancestral Hall** immediately to the south dates from the early 16th century. Both buildings consist of three halls connected by two internal courtyards. Ancestral tablets of entire generations or of individual family members are displayed inside. Large assembly halls of this kind are used not only for the important purposes of ancestor worship, but also as places for family celebrations and meetings.

Lying in a more remote location, the **Yeung Hau Temple** was built in honour of Hau Wong, a general of the Song Dynasty (960–1279) who protected the two last remaining child emperors of the defeated imperial dynasty after their flight to the south.

Yeung Hau Temple, interior

Beyond an old well lies the walled village of **Sheung Cheung Wai**. Only a few remnants of the old village still exist, as within the walled compound new houses have been built and old ones converted, but this is very much a living village. Outside the fortification, a traditional **Altar to the Earth God** has been restored. It is a small platform, on which a stone represents the earth deity.

The last monument on the trail is the hexagonal **Tsui Shing Lau Pagoda**, which dates from the 14th or 15th century. It is 42ft (13m) tall with three storeys, each bearing a name related to the stars. Built to ward off bad *feng shui* influences, it originally nestled between woods and a small lake. Today, it stands forlorn against the concrete backdrop of Tin Shui Wai's housing estates.

Tsui Shing Lau Pagoda

Taxi is the easiest way to reach the final stop on this tour, **San Tin village**, which is situated between Yuen Long and Sheung Shui. However, the energetic and determined should be able to make it there by public transport in two hops by taking the LRT to the Fung Nin Road or Hong Lok Road stop in Yuen Long and boarding a maxicab No 75 or 76 from Fook Hong Street.

Tai Fu Tai

The main attraction in San Tin is ★★ **Tai Fu Tai** (9am to 1pm and 2pm to 5pm, except Tuesday and some public holidays) in Wing Ping Tsuen hamlet. This gracious residence was built in 1865 for Man Cheung-luen, an official whom the emperor honoured with the title *dai fu* (*tai fu* in Cantonese). Freely translated, the name of the house means 'House of the Great Master', and it truly lives up to its name.

The owner's portrait hangs above the altar opposite the entrance, flanked by pictures of his first wife and his eldest son on the right and his second wife and third son on the left. Two plaques record compliments received by Man Cheung-luen from the imperial court on passing the civil service entrance examination. In accordance with regulations passed by the Manchurian Qing Dynasty, which ruled China until 1911, the inscriptions, like those on all official documents, are written in Manchurian as well as Chinese.

The living apartments lead off from a central courtyard, as do the bedrooms on the first floor. The servants lived in a wing off to one side of the main building, where the kitchen had previously been situated on the right-hand side. On the way to the kitchen quarters there is a hollow tree trunk which was used for pressing oil from groundnuts.

Apart from the main fireplace in the kitchen there are seven smaller ones. The reason for this, according to legend, is that Man Cheung-luen had seven sons and when they married they all continued to live in the house with their respective wives. The seven daughters-in-law were unable to agree with each other about any domestic arrangements, so it was decided that, in the interests of harmony, they should each have their own fireplace. On the right-hand side is a corridor leading to the rear entrance of the house and to an attractive garden.

A 10-minute walk past Tai Fu Tai brings you to Fan Tin Tsuen hamlet and the 17th-century ★ **Man Lun Fung Ancestral Hall**, where the Mans have venerated their ancestors since the 17th century.

Going home

The quickest way back to Kowloon or Central from San Tin is to take a No 76K bus or taxi to Sheung Shui KCR station and proceed by train as far as the MTR interchange at Kowloon Tong.

Outlying Islands

Lantau Island

Almost twice the size of Hong Kong, yet largely rural in character, ★★**Lantau** was once an island of tranquility, spiritual retreats and small fishing communities. Today, Hong Kong International Airport stands at Chek Lap Kok on the northwest coastline, the population has swelled from 20,000 to over 200,000 people, a major New Town development has engulfed the sleepy coastal village of Tung Chung, and there are plans for a major port development (and possibly a Disneyland) in the north. But even then, a day trip to the fishing village of Tai O and to the hilly plain dominated by Po Lin Monastery should provide a welcome respite from life in the jungle of the big city.

Tai O

To get there, catch a ferry from Central Ferry Pier No 7 to **Mui Wo**, whose English name is Silvermine Bay. The eponymous mine, however, closed long ago. The village itself is unremarkable, so nothing will prevent visitors from immediately boarding the No 1 bus waiting at the bus station in front of the pier. It takes 40 minutes to reach Tai O at the other end of the island.

Just out of Silvermine Bay, the road starts to climb the first hills, which are typical of the landscape on this large island. On the way to Pui O, it passes the start of several hiking trails in **North Lantau Country Park**, many of them leading towards Sunset Peak, at 2,781ft (869m), the second-highest mountain on Lantau.

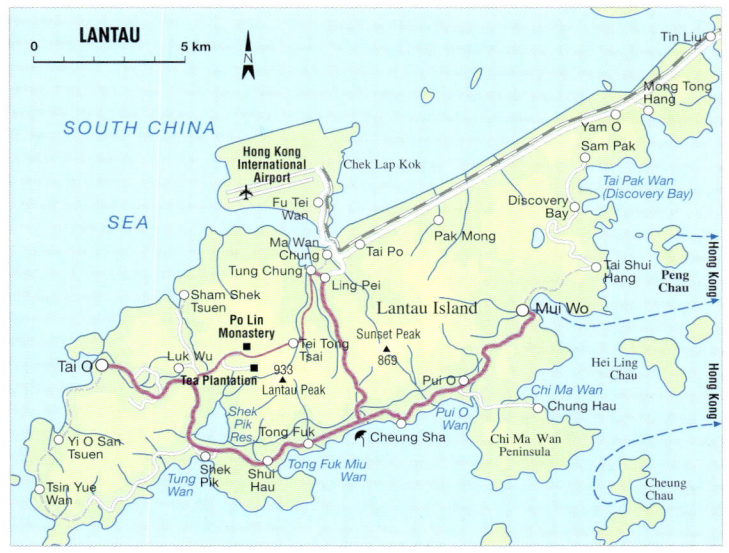

Numerous picnic and grill places border the road. **Pui O** is a small village with large numbers of holiday apartments provided by Hong Kong firms for the use of their employees at the weekends and during short annual vacations. The little beach is not particularly attractive. From here the road leads off to **Chi Ma Wan Peninsula**, where, in rough countryside, archaeologists have found lime kilns and relics from the Bronze Age which show that the islands and the South China Coast must have been settled from early times.

Visitors intending to include an interlude on the beach in their itinerary should stop off at the 2-mile (3-km) ★ **Cheung Sha Upper Beach**. This is Hong Kong's largest beach and even at the weekend it is relatively empty, and the water is fairly clean. Changing rooms and showers are available during the April to October swimming season. There are also a couple of local seafood restaurants on the beach.

The government takes advantage of the remoteness of Lantau to keep one of the most difficult types of crime under control. On the slope behind Tong Fuk there are several prisons and reform centres for drug addicts, and there is another in Tung Wan, below Shek Pik reservoir. The bus route crosses the 173-ft (54-m) dam. The drinking water is pumped through a pipeline to Hong Kong Island. From the reservoir visitors will get their first glimpse of the big Buddha statue at Po Lin Monastery.

Beyond the reservoir the bus slows down somewhat as the road climbs steeply, giving passengers plenty of time to study the surrounding mountains. After crossing the pass, the road runs downhill into the fertile Tai O plain. On the slopes are perched several little monasteries with fine views across the lowlands.

Tired cyclist at Tai O

During the last century, what is now the sleepy fishing village of ★ **Tai O** was of great importance for the island. Lying on the north coast of Lantau, it overlooks the Pearl River Estuary. Further upriver lies Guangzhou, which as the city of Canton was the most important trading and economic centre in South China. It had its own viceroy and was also the only port at which foreign traders were permitted to disembark. The population of Tai O, by contrast, was primarily employed in fishing and the salt industry, two important and profitable economic spheres at the time. They still play a part in the economy today, although rice farming, duck raising and the manufacture of shrimp paste provide a broader basis, a fact which can be smelt as you cross the village.

Dried fish stall, Tai O

From the end of the car park where the buses stop, turn right into the main street, along which every third shop seems to sell dried or pickled fish. In traditional houses

Tai O – a village clinging to its past

there are no clearly defined boundaries between shop and house; the family may be sitting at the back and eating, or the children perched on a wooden bench in front of the television set. At night, some family members will retire to the first floor to sleep, whilst the others put up their camp beds in the shop. Many of the doors are still adorned with traditional posters of watchmen, or have the guardian figures painted directly onto the doors. In quite a number of the houses, decorative tiles or ceramic figures can also be seen.

Parallel to the main road, a creek separates the main island from the little offshore island of Fu Shan. Until 1996, the channel was traversed by a flat punt which was pulled backwards and forwards by two elderly women. This has been replaced by a Chinese pagoda-style drawbridge, which provides a good view of the settlement of rather ramshackle, metal-sheeted **stit houses** rising out of the mud. For some, this kind of dwelling represents the best alternative to living on a boat, but the government apparently thinks differently and has slated these traditional houses for demolition. New accommodation has already been built, but many – particularly the older residents – are extremely reluctant to leave.

It's worth walking past the stilt houses to the ★ **Hau Wong Temple** built on a narrow spit of land surrounded by water. Dating from 1699, this is the oldest of four temples in the territory dedicated to Yang Liang-je, an uncle of the last two Song dynasty emperors, who as boys sought refuge from the Mongols on Lantau when the latter invaded the empire at the end of the 13th century.

Head back towards the market place at the heart of the village. Notice how dried fish makes up a large percentage of the goods on offer. On the market square lies **Kwan Tai Temple**, dedicated to the god of war and justice. Within

The bottle garden Hau Wong Temple

the triple-winged building, whose interior is black with smoke, are a number of wooden figures and simple stones before which the faithful offer incense sticks or fruit.

From Tai O, the next destination should be the ★★ **Po Lin Monastery**, situated at Ngong Ping in the glorious upland scenery of central Lantau. The cheapest way to get there is by bus: the No 21 leaves every hour for Ngong Ping on the hour between 11am and 3pm from Tai O bus stop. Taxis can also usually be found waiting here.

Po Lin Monastery gate

Visitors at the incense burner

The first monks settled on the high plateau of Ngong Ping in 1905. When their numbers increased following the founding of the Chinese Republic in 1912, the Po Lin Monastery was officially dedicated in 1927. Until the 1970s it was an almost unknown, remote complex, but nowadays the monks and nuns have mastered the art of temple tourism quite well. The building projects within the temple boundaries prove that the amount of money from donations has increased. It used to be possible to stay overnight at the monastery until the government discovered that the enterprising brethren had no licence to conduct such business. All that remains of their hospitality is the **Chinese vegetarian lunch** which can be eaten in the refectory following the purchase of computerised place-allocation tickets (there are two set menus on offer at HK$100 or HK$60).

The temple area of the monastery follows the traditional plan and architecture of Chinese Buddhist temples. All the important buildings lie one behind the other on a single axis. Their conspicuous roofs have upturned eaves, and the principal ones stand on high platforms. In the first hall, visitors are greeted by the portly, laughing figure of Milefo. He represents the 10th-century monk Qi Ci, who at his death revealed himself to be an incarnation of Maitreya, the Buddha of the Future. He is surrounded by four heavenly guardians, one for each point of the compass. Behind Milefo stands Weito, the messenger of the gods.

Between the entrance hall and the main temple pavilion is a line of large bronze vessels for incense sticks, and two tablets symbolising the Wheel of Life flank the entrance staircase, which affords an attractive view of the surroundings. In the main pavilion, three gilt Buddha statues adorn the altar: in the middle is Sakyamuni, the historical Buddha, to the left the Buddha of the Past and to the right the Healing Buddha. Prayer flags hang from the roof, and carved wooden frames support the drum and bell, both symbols of time.

Buddhist nun

The rooms at the rear serve the monks and nuns for private meditation and study. Occasionally, visitors are allowed a glimpse of a very small and extremely valuable Burmese Buddha statue made of white jade.

At the other end of the scale is the huge **bronze Buddha** opposite the temple, weighing in at 202 tonnes and claimed to be the world's largest outdoor seated Buddha. Planning began in 1974, but a succession of problems held up production and the official dedication ceremony was not held until 29 December 1993. A staircase of 268 steps leads up to the statue, symbolising the merit Buddhists must earn in this life in preparation for the next. At the top is the Tian Tan, the 'Altar of Heaven', on which the Buddha sits on a bed of lotus. In the Buddhist religion the lotus symbolises purity, for it grows in muddy pools and still brings forth pure white flowers.

Inside the altar is a valuable wooden statue of the Bodhisattva Khsitigarbha made of very hard *nanmu* wood. A bronze bell weighing 6 tonnes and engraved with Buddhist inscriptions is rung 108 times every morning, with a computer to control the 'lucky' number of chimes. There are oil paintings depicting the life of the Buddha. It is also believed that relics of the Buddha are preserved here. Bearing in mind that the Buddha was cremated soon after his death and that a number of temples also claim to own relics, a certain amount of scepticism may be called for.

Bronze Buddha and visitors

Monastery: interior sculpture

A footpath leads off from the roundabout past Hong Kong's only **Tea Plantation** – which was established in 1959 by a Briton – before climbing steeply to the top of Hong Kong's second tallest mountain, ★ **Lantau Peak** (3,064ft/934m) for spectacular panoramic views.

The next destination, **Tung Chung**, can be reached in under 50 minutes by the No 23 bus (10 and 40 minutes past the hour until 5.10pm; 6.10pm and 7.10pm; more frequent on Sunday and public holidays). There is also a concrete footpath providing you have the energy, and at least 1 ½ hours to spare.

From here you can choose to head straight back to Kowloon or Hong Kong Island by MTR (30 minutes), or linger a while to visit the early 19th-century Chinese ★ **Tung Chung Fort** (information centre 9am to 4pm except Tuesday and public holidays). The fort was constructed in 1832, and it was the base from which the Chinese army controlled coastal shipping until the British leased Lantau in 1898. At the end of the 1930s the local residents used the fort as a school, until the arrival of the Japanese forces. There is an exhibition room in which a display of photographs documents the history of the complex.

From here, you can savour the almost surreal juxtaposition of Tung Chung 'old village', with its traditional stilt houses and picturesque ★ **Hau Wong Temple**, against the backdrop of **Hong Kong International Airport** at Chek Lap Kok.

Cheung Chau harbour

Cheung Chau and Lamma

During the week, life on the smaller islands in the shadow of Lantau continues at a gentle and unhurried pace. Come weekends, however, the ferries disgorge hordes of day trippers who flock to the beaches and occupy the little weekend guest rooms. Therefore, if you can manage to, it is preferable to choose a quiet weekday for your visit.

It will take about 2 hours to visit the temple and market village of ★★ **Cheung Chau** or to walk from one ferry port to the other on the island of ★ **Lamma**. On both islands your visit can be rounded off at a seafood restaurant with views out across the sea.

Both of these outings commence with a trip on one of the regular ferries which make the crossing between the islands and the Central Ferry Piers (Pier No 6 for Cheung Chau; Pier No 5 for Lamma).

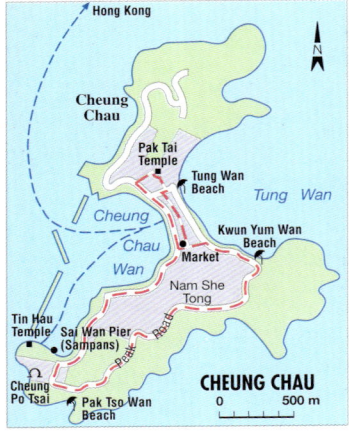

Cheung Chau

The quay at Cheung Chau juts out from the bustling waterfront promenade. Head left along the **Praya** (harbour promenade), which affords a good view of life on the junks and little sampans in the bay. Soon you will reach the first restaurants on **Pak She Praya Road**, where you can make your choice as to where to stop off later on. You'll come to a sports ground, behind which stands ★★ **Pak Tai Temple**, which dates from 1783.

Pak Tai is the Cantonese name for the Ruler of the North. According to legend, he received from the Jade Emperor, the highest Taoist deity, the command over 12 heavenly legions in order to fight the King of Demons, who had among his forces a grey tortoise and a giant snake. Of course, Pak Tai was victorious over the forces of evil. He is usually represented in a sitting position, with his feet resting on a tortoise and a snake.

In 1777, when the plague had broken out on Cheung Chau, the islanders fetched the local Pak Tai statue from their native village on the mainland (according to one version of the legend, local fishermen found the statue floating in the sea). However it came there, the island was spared further visitations by the pestilence from this time onwards, so a temple was built out of gratitude for the divine intervention. The statue is flanked by the dark figures of Thousand-Li-Eye and Good-Wind-Ear, two popular figures from Chinese mythology who are famous for their remarkable sensory powers.

Pak Tai figures

Each year in May, the colourful ★★ **Bun Festival** is held in front of the temple. It dates back to the discovery of human bones during construction work, which led the inhabitants to fear that the temple would be haunted by the spirits which had been disturbed. In order to appease them, they put out offerings of steamed buns. Today, the event is celebrated by the erection of three 52-ft (16-m) high bamboo towers, each piled with some 5,000 pink and white lotus paste buns. Religious groups set up stands in which deities and temple paintings are displayed during the festival. The festival lasts for about nine days, and for three of them the islanders become strict vegetarians. Chinese opera, lion dances and musical performances take place on the square. Statues from all the wayside and village temples on the island are carried to Pak Tai Temple.

The highlight of the festival is the ★★ **grand procession** in which the statues are returned to their homes accompanied by a brightly-coloured procession with floats, banners and dragon dances. The key characters in the procession are always portrayed by children, who wear colourful, traditional costumes. They are carried along the route on concealed poles, borne by the stronger participants, and whether kneeling or standing they remain, like dolls, absolutely still, apparently 'floating' above the heads of the spectators.

The Bun Festival procession

Until recently, the morning after the procession was also marked by the ritual of young men climbing the towers and retrieving as many buns as possible. The one who accumulated the most buns from the highest points on the tower would enjoy the best *joss* during the following year. The inherent dangers of the climb, however, forced the abandonment of the practice, and now, to the dismay of some people who don't like to see the old ways disappear, the buns are collected in a more orderly manner and distributed among the inhabitants.

Windsurfers at Kwun Wan Yam

Altar to the Earth Deity

Café at Kwun Yam Wan

From the temple, walk down Pak She Street. At the next crossroads, the intersection with Kwok Man Road, there is a little **Altar to the Earth Deity** on the left which is always adorned with incense sticks and offerings. In former times, these simple animist shrines on which the earth deity is represented only by a stone, could be seen in virtually every district. They bear witness to the wide variety of Chinese religious beliefs and the differing levels of abstraction involved.

Diagonally opposite is San Hing Street, lined with typical village shops and leading straight into the alleys of the bustling ★ **market quarter**. Here you will find traditional village hats, Chinese medicines, dried foodstuffs and joss sticks on sale alongside modern household goods. At the end turn left along Tung Wun Road to the sandy **Tung Wan** and **Kwun Yam Wan beaches**.

The bay is very popular with windsurfers, and the **Cheung Chau Windsurfing Centre and Café** (tel: 2981 8316) owned by the uncle of windsurfing champion and 1996 Olympic gold medalist Lee Lai-shan ('San-san') provides lessons as well as equipment rentals. The centre is at the south end of the bay, past the modern **Warwick Hotel**. This is Cheung Chau's poshest hotel and if you feel like treating yourself it is a possible choice for an overnight stay (you may get a room without booking during the week, but make reservations in advance for weekend visits, tel: 2981 0081).

The path leads below the hotel, passing a 3,000-year-old, geometric **rock carving**, rediscovered in 1970.

If you want a longer walk around the southern part of the island, follow Kwun Yam Wan Road up the hill behind the hotel to **Peak Road**. Head south and follow Peak Road until you come to a cemetery and then a path down to **Pak Tso Wan** beach. Further around the promontory is the

Cheung Po Tsai cave, where a notorious Ching dynasty pirate allegedly buried his treasure; and an old **Tin Hau temple**.

Return to the ferry pier by sampan from Sai Wan village or continue round the coast on the wide road that leads back to the waterfront. Turn right just before you reach the covered market for dinner at **Lotus Thai**, or head back to one of the seafood restaurants on the Praya.

Lamma

Lamma has a reputation for great seafood restaurants and the 'alternative' lifestyle of some of its expatriate community. This walk gives you a taste of both. Start by boarding a Yung Shue Wan-bound ferry from Central Pier No 5. When you get there, follow Yung Shue Wan Main Street round the harbour past the open-air Chinese restaurants, grocery shops, gift shops and cafés serving Western food. The **Bookworm Café**, or a traditional *dim sum* at the **Sampan** restaurant are good bets for a late breakfast or light lunch. There is a well-tended **Tin Hau Temple** behind the sports field past the Bookworm Café.

After strolling through the village, you should follow signposts to **Hung Shing Ye**. As the modern tiled houses gradually peter out, the path winds past small vegetable plots and dotted hamlets, with the three chimneys of Lamma Power Station looming ever-present on your right. **Hung Shing Ye Beach** is relatively clean, with changing rooms, snack stalls and a hotel café.

At the far end of the beach the narrow concrete path starts to climb more steeply, and leads, after a few sharp bends, to a hill with an observation pavilion. This marks the halfway point of the walk. From here the path descends into **Lo So Shing**, a sleepy hamlet of traditional Chinese houses. From here you can either follow the signs to pretty ★ **Lo So Shing Beach** or continue directly to **Sok Kwu Wan** (Picnic Bay).

The north side of the bay is scarred by a quarry and cement works. The bay itself is used for intensive fish farming. Much of the produce is used to stock the fish tanks of the ★★ **seafood restaurants** that line the waterfront on the south side of the bay. These are what makes Lamma such a popular destination for local residents at weekends and holidays. Customers can choose their meal from the tanks or from the menu – deep fried squid, minced quail and steamed garlic or peppered prawns are popular choices with local expats, who tend to avoid shellfish because of the Hepatitis A risk factor. There are ferries back to Central every two hours or so; or you can ask the restaurant staff about taking a kaido or sampan to Aberdeen.

Lamma: fishermen's stilt houses

Locals chat in the sun

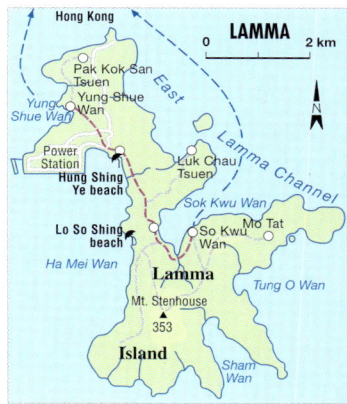

Religion and Superstition

Among the most modern cities in the world, with advanced technology, innovative building design and every modern convenience, Hong Kong is culturally still very much a Chinese city. This is evident not only in the calligraphy of the street and shop signs, the locals practising *tai chi* in the parks, taking their songbirds for walks or playing *mahjong*, but also in the numerous temples and shrines to be found all over the territory.

East Asian beliefs are very different from those in the West. They rest on the twin pillars of Confucianism, which covers all public matters, and Taoism, which provides the individual creed. These two philosophies permeate everyday life despite the fact that they are radically opposed to each other and create a strong sphere of conflict in day-to-day behaviour, in which individuals must seek their own personal synthesis. Not only do Confucianism and Taoism furnish the basis for religion; they also explain traditional family celebrations, public festivals and a wide range of symbolic acts.

Unlike Christianity, Confucianism and Taoism have no church, and therefore no institution to govern, regulate and dogmatise faith. Religion is a very private affair with which everyone must come to terms alone. However, the religious aspect is only one small element in the wide-ranging philosophies of the East, and it has very little to do with original thoughts. Instead, it is surrounded by a network of legends and myths, with simple ceremonies and colourful spectacles to guarantee its universal appeal.

Confucius (551–479BC) was the son of a minor nobleman in what is today the province of Shandong. He lived in unruly times, and wanted to become an advisor to a princely court in order to present to the ruler his thoughts on peace and order. In doing so he referred to the 'ideal rulers' Yao and Shun, whose only disadvantage was that their origins lay in the world of mythology. The state declared the theories of Confucius to be largely idealistic. Confucius saw the 'ideal' society as consisting of a strict hierarchy in which rulers had the power to make decisions for ministers, fathers for sons, husbands for wives and older brothers for younger ones. Only relationships between friends were regarded as equal. In return, the rulers were required to treat their subjects with benevolence and to care for them. The 'school' of Confucius had virtually no influence during his lifetime and the Master was denied a high position and had to eke out an existence as a wandering tutor. His pupils, however, achieved considerable influence and, in their position as princely advisors, developed the theory of the 'mandate

Opposite: A Buddha among Ten Thousand

Mahjong in progress

Religion is a private affair

of Heaven', which was to legitimise the ruler's claim to power. During the Han Dynasty (206BC–220AD), the emperor was so convinced by the doctrines of Confucius that he added paragraphs concerning the maintenance of power and declared them to be the national doctrine. The effects can still be observed in some East Asian countries where societies are characterised by lack of social mobility, and authoritarian regimes govern the political scene.

Strong family ties emanate from the respect due to one's ancestors, a duty instilled into the eldest son. It is believed that the soul leaves the body at death but finds no rest for three generations, haunting and influencing the lives of those left behind. In order to ensure that the soul is contented it must be given those things which it needed during its earthly life. On special days set aside for paying tribute to one's ancestors, fake paper money is burned on the grave or in the temple, borne by smoke into the spirit world. The souls thus acquire god-like status: both are revered but not worshipped. Neither the souls of the departed nor the gods are seen as capable of human action, and the tablets devoted to ancestors or figures of divinities are seen as memorials or means of concentration.

Ancestral Hall

This belief provides the link to Taoism, which concentrates exclusively on the individual and his ability to find his individual *Tao*, in other words an attitude which is at one with his nature. The Taoist often finds this in the behaviour pattern known as the *wu wei*, which is frequently translated as 'way'. This is a form of non-interference which should not be seen as passivity but which involves activity in harmony with nature.

The development of Taoism is ascribed to the hermit Lao Tzu (c 6th century BC), although there is evidence that the *Tao Te Ching* ('The Way and the Virtue') is a later collection of aphorisms. Closely linked to Taoism is the idea of *yin* and *yang*, two opposing forces which each bear the essence of the other within them and which find balance in a perfect synthesis. The *yang* stands for masculinity, strength, hardness, brightness, heat, activity and the south; the *yin* is the symbol of femininity, weakness, softness, darkness, cold, passivity and the north.

Yin and yang symbols

The influence of Taoism in art cannot be overestimated. Painters, calligraphers and poets were limited by clearly laid-down traditions regarding technique and subject, but in the execution of their art and their attitude to life they devoted themselves to Taoism. The scenes depicted in the typical landscape paintings on rice paper were copied time and time again and reveal Taoist thoughts. Vast precipitous mountains swathed in clouds dominate the picture in which human figures are insignificant. Nature is seen as the all-powerful element in which man should seek his place without contradiction as far as this is possible.

Taoism, like Confucianism, was originally not a religion. It developed its popular forms only after the arrival of Buddhism in China, i.e. in about 65AD. Mahayana Buddhism, or the Way of the Greater Vehicle, spread throughout China. This doctrine proclaims that deliverance and entry into nirvana as a release from all earthly suffering can also be achieved with the assistance of the *bodhisattvas*. These are Buddhist saints who postpone their own enlightenment in order to help others. The best-known *bodhisattva* is Avalokiteshvara, who underwent a gender transformation in China to become Guanyin (Kwun Yum or Kwun Yam in Cantonese), the much-loved Goddess of Mercy.

Taoism also acquired a vast pantheon of gods. Pride of place is occupied by the Jade Emperor, followed by divinities of lesser importance. The second level is occupied by the Eight Immortals, originally historic personages of the 7th–10th century about whom legends later grew, relating the ways in which they achieved their immortality. The Eight Immortals live on the Island of the Blessed and can return to earth to help mankind in a similar manner to the *bodhisattvas*. The seven men and one woman each possess a characteristic sign by which they can be recognised and which will frequently be spotted in stylised form adorning the poles in the temples of Hong Kong: a fly-swatter, a gourd, a basket of flowers, etc. The third level is occupied by earthly beings who are revered as if they were gods. Most of these are historic personages such as poets, doctors, officials and generals who distinguished themselves in some way and who later acquired legendary status. There are vast numbers of them, most only being known on a local or regional level. Hong Kong's best-loved Taoist divinity is Tin Hau, the patroness of fishermen and sailors. She occupies the highest level as the Queen of Heaven.

The Taoist philosophy of nature also gave rise to the geomancy known in Hong Kong as *feng shui*, literally translated as 'wind-water'. *Feng shui* asserts that buildings should also harmonise with their surroundings, that they should be protected and should have no sharp corners. The most favourable location for a building is with a mountain behind, if possible to the north. The south and the front side of the building should open onto a plain. The explanation is simple and practical: the ideas arose in north China, where icy winds and sandstorms from the Mongolian plains blow down from the north, and where having a protective mountain makes sense. A mountain to the south, on the other hand, would block out the sun which is as essential for life as water. Apart from influencing the site of residential buildings, the principles of *feng shui* are used to position the graves of ancestors. Since the in-

Painting in Miu Fat Temple

Stone lions divert bad currents

fluence of ancestors on the living is so crucial, it is essential that they should be laid to rest in the most favourable location.

This original idea has given way to countless stories and myths, including that of a dragon which supposedly lives in every mountain. This is an area where the Chinese are masters of pragmatism – especially those who live in Hong Kong, where the most favourable locations for buildings are often compromised by the shortage of land. Minor constructional additions, like a strategically placed fountain or a stone lion, can divert bad currents; mirrors can drive away evil spirits. The *feng shui* experts are masters at finding ways and means of justifying an exception to the rule. It should not be assumed, however, that everyone in Hong Kong believes implicitly in all these stories. They are symbols which remind the community of its roots and encourage communication in an utterly practical manner. Some manifestations – like the hole in the wall of the building in Repulse Bay – are simply publicity stunts, and very good ones at that, for every tourist is familiar with the story.

The significance of numbers also makes an interesting game. In many societies, the number 8 is a lucky number, because it can be repeated an infinite number of times without removing the pen from the paper. In China, too, the number 8 symbolises infinity and eternal life. It is thus not a coincidence that the Tao immortals are eight in number. In Hong Kong, moreover, the Cantonese names for several numbers sound similar to words with completely different meanings. Thus, the word for 'one' is associated with the word for 'must', 'two' is linked to 'easy' or 'light' and the word for 'eight' to 'excess'. Only the number 4 is a bad omen, for the Cantonese word for it sounds like that for 'death'. People have made up an infinite variety of ways to support this superstition; for example, Hong Kong citizens may make sure that their car registration plates consist only of 'good' numbers. Number 28 could be taken to mean 'win excess easily' or, better still, a quadrupling of the number of excess: '8888'. Most prestigious of all are the one-digit numbers. The government shrewdly auctions such numbers and uses the income to finance social projects.

Number combinations containing the number '4', on the other hand, are avoided. Worst of all is '14', for it means 'must die'. For this reason, many buildings have no 14th floor as no one would want to live on this level. Sometimes, the number '13' is also missing in order to appease Western superstitions. The most auspicious day of this century was, of course, 8.8.88, a day on which the registry offices had to put in overtime performing marriage ceremonies, and countless new businesses were founded.

Festivals and Folklore

Dazzling effigies

Traditional festivals are a natural product of religious and superstitious beliefs and mostly honour individual gods or ancestors. They follow the ancient Chinese lunar calendar and the cycle begins with the New Year's festival on the first full moon between mid-January and mid-February. Families spring-clean their homes, buy new furnishings or possessions, redecorate – especially with 'lucky' pictures of fish, because, like certain numbers, the words 'luck' and 'fish' are near homonyms. Above all, the ancestral altar must be cleaned, as according to legend, the Kitchen God ascends to heaven on the eve of the New Year to give the Jade Emperor a report on the family. In order to ensure that he tells only the sweetest stories, some Chinese smear the mouth of his image with honey.

According to Confucian tradition, superiors must show their subordinates their goodwill at **Chinese New Year**. Nowadays, this usually involves *lai see*, or gifts of 'lucky' money in little red envelopes, red being the colour of good fortune. Children, unmarried relatives and junior workers will be remembered on this occasion. People wish each other *kung hei fat choi*, or much prosperity and success in the new lunar year. The festival itself, however, is spent at home feasting and celebrating with the family. Many take the opportunity to visit relatives across the border, and the city grinds to a halt for several days. Previously, vast firework displays would chase away the evil spirits. Today, however, the law is victorious over tradition, and private firework displays are banned on safety grounds. By way of compensation, the government sends a few millions' worth of fireworks rocketing into the air above the harbour every year.

Officially, the end of New Year festivities is marked on the 15th day with the **Spring Lantern Festival** (Yuen

Chinese New Year – a time for giving and celebrating

Siu), which is a Chinese equivalent of Valentine's Day. Much more important is the **Ching Ming Festival** in April, when thousands of people visit the cemeteries to pay respect to their ancestors by cleaning the graves, lighting incense and offering gifts.

Although the **Tin Hau Festival** celebrating the goddess' birthday on the 23rd day of the third lunar month (April/May) is not an official holiday, it is marked by numerous processions in which the statues of the goddess are carried through the streets or, more appropriately, loaded into boats for a ceremonial patrol of the bays dotting the coastline. There are dragon dances, local opera performances and many other spectacles.

Cheung Chau Bun Festival (April/May, also not a public holiday) is celebrated with processions, dragon dances, etc., when spirits whose bones were disturbed during the construction of the Pak Tai Temple are appeased with offerings of steamed buns. See pages 58–9 for more details of this colourful event.

The religious origins of the **Tuen Ng Dragon Boat Festival** are obscure, although ceremonies to dedicate the boats mark the start of the proceedings. The story surrounding the festival is that during the Zhou Dynasty (1122–221BC), a loyal official, Qu Yuan, commited suicide by throwing himself into the river when his suggested reforms were rejected. Too late to save him, fishermen threw rice dumplings into the water to prevent the fish from eating his body. The incident is marked by eating glutinous rice cakes filled with meat called *zhongzi*, and holding boat races. The **International Dragon Boat Races** take place after Tuen Ng, and have become an important event in the sporting calendar, with teams from 15 countries participating. The races are held at Sha Tin in June or July, depending on the lunar calendar.

Dragon Boat Festival

Local people burn paper offerings outside their shops and homes to placate lost souls during the **Hungry Ghost Festival** in August. This is not a public holiday.

Mid-Autumn Festival, also known as the Moon or Lantern Festival, is held during the September full moon. It is a sort of harvest festival, during which sweet delicacies called mooncakes, with a bean paste and egg filling, are eaten. Families gather with brightly coloured lanterns in public spaces (parks, beaches, hilltops) to watch the full moon. A second ritual cleaning of ancestors' graves (see Ching Ming, above, for the first) takes place a few weeks later at the October **Chung Yeung Festival**.

Traditional Chinese music is actively encouraged by the administration to ensure that it reaches the general public. There are occasional performances of Chinese opera, but these are mostly part of the temple festivals.

Western Culture

The metropolis has plenty to offer in the field of contemporary high-rise architecture. Sir Norman Foster used bridge-building techniques in his Hong Kong and Shanghai Bank, whilst I.M. Pei chose a series of triangular surfaces for his famous landmark, the **Bank of China**, the second tallest building in Hong Kong and the seventh tallest in the world at 1,209 ft (369m). Enthusiasts for tall buildings will also appreciate Hong Kong's tallest (and the world's sixth tallest), **Central Plaza** in Wanchai (1,227ft/374m). A more recent addition to the skyline is Hong Kong's third (and the world's eighth) tallest building, the 1,149ft (350m) **Center** in Sheung Wan. **Hong Kong International Airport** is a beautiful structure, and the HK Airport Core Programme has been voted one of the ten greatest architectural/engineering achievements of the 20th century.

Architecture is the most visible manifestation of Western culture in Hong Kong. A search for the performing arts is rather more difficult. The government is devoting much energy to the organisation of festivals in an attempt to disprove the city's reputation as a purely commercial centre. Despite wide public interest, however, these events often seem artificial.

The **City Festival** (January/February) organised by the Fringe Club offers an eclectic programme of contemporary arts that acts as a curtain raiser the **Hong Kong Arts Festival** (February/March). The City (or Fringe) Festival has traditionally offered more avant-garde and experimental performances while the Arts Festival attracts more established musicians, dancers and theatrical performers from the world circuit.

It will come as no surprise to learn that Hong Kong, as a centre of the film-making industry, should also have its own **International Film Festival** (March/April). More than 100 films from all over the world are presented over a two-week period. These are likely to include two or three premieres, usually of Chinese films. Retrospectives, special themes and exhibitions complete the festival.

Modern art is a more complicated affair. Since the 1950s, Hong Kong artists have used the conflict between Eastern and Western culture creatively to discover new ways of presenting their ideas. Initially scorned by Hong Kong society, their works are now displayed in the Hong Kong Museum of Art as well as in public buildings such as the Cultural Centre.

There are hundreds of commercial art galleries in Hong Kong. Many of them close almost as quickly as they open, but the local papers and listings magazines provide details of current exhibitions.

Wanchai from the harbour

Academy for Performing Arts

Food and Drink

Opposite: seafood assortment

The ethnic melting pot of Hong Kong has created a gourmet's paradise, offering what is generally accepted to be the best Chinese food in the world. Apart from the various Chinese cuisines described below, food from neighbouring Asian countries – Thai, Japanese, Korean, Indian and Vietnamese – is also found in abundance and is of excellent quality. Western cuisine is well represented by restaurants in the more expensive hotels and in numerous chic eateries concentrated in areas such as Lan Kwai Fong, SoHo (South of Hollywood Road), Causeway Bay and Knutsford Terrace in Tsim Sha Tsui.

Dim sum/Yum cha

Dim sum

One of Hong Kong's traditional delicacies is *yum cha* ('drink tea') or *dim sum* (literally 'little hearts'), little snacks originally served with tea at breakfast, but which today are more popular as a light lunch. Most *dim sum* are small savoury appetisers made of dough, filled with vegetables, meat or seafood, and steamed in bamboo baskets over boiling water. However, *dim sum* can also include deep-fried spring rolls, sweet cakes and the more exotic braised chicken's feet. In traditional *dim sum* restaurants, waiting staff push around trolleys from which guests help themselves to whatever dishes take their fancy. Each plate taken is marked on a card and added to the bill. In some restaurants, *dim sum* menus have replaced the trolleys, making it more difficult to decide what to eat.

Cantonese cuisine

Down at the market

Your favourite Chinese restaurant back home is most likely to serve Cantonese cuisine as the region around Guangzhou is where many Chinese emigrants originated. Many Chinese restaurants in Europe and the USA have adapted their food to appeal to local residents, but generally, native Cantonese cuisine does not overpower the senses with the use of pungent sauces or spices. As in any coastal province, fish and other seafood are popular ingredients, usually steamed or braised very quickly and served with a simple soy-based sauce. Be very cautious about local shellfish, however, as there is a real risk of heavy metals poisoning and Hepatitis A. Large coral fish may also be contaminated with cyanide traces. Chicken and pork are the most popular types of meat used in Cantonese dishes. An innumerable variety of green leafy vegetables are eaten, usually briefly stir-fried in a wok with oyster sauce. In a typical Cantonese meal, steamed white rice is always the staple, accompanied by an array of side dishes, usually a soup, a meat or seafood dish and a vegetable stir fry.

Speciality dishes, using rare ingredients believed to have fortifying effects, are usually reserved for wedding celebrations and other festive occasions. Shark's fin, said to be an aphrodisiac, is prepared as soup; abalone, a type of shellfish, is claimed to be strengthening; bird's nests, purported to ease asthmatic attacks, utilise the saliva which swallows produce to bind their nests together on the cliffs. All these specialities are extremely expensive.

Dried produce

Other Chinese cuisines

In the cuisine of Northern China, noodles and steamed rolls accompany most meals rather than rice because wheat is a major crop on the northern plains. Filled dumplings (*jiaozi*) are a popular speciality. Another well-loved dish in is Peking Duck. The name refers to the special manner of preparation: the skin of the bird is inflated like a balloon and basted with a special marinade before it is roasted in a very hot oven. When cooked, the crispy skin, but not the meat, is sliced into bite-sized pieces and served with a thin pancake, fresh scallions and *hoisin* sauce. The duck meat is used to cook other dishes accompanying the meal.

Advance orders must be placed for Beggar's Chicken, which is stuffed with cabbage and spices and wrapped in lotus leaves before it is encased in clay and baked for several hours. The waiter smashes the clay casing at the guest's table, making a great show of it and releasing the aromas of the now very tender bird.

The Mongolian grill also originated in the north. Choose your ingredients from a buffet and either give them to the chef to cook or prepare them yourself on a hotplate at the table. Or you can opt for the fondue-like Mongolian fire pot, in which meat, seafood, tofu, chopped vegetables and other ingredients are cooked in boiling stock. The food is retrieved using chopsticks or little wire baskets.

Preparing prawns
A soup vendor

The southwestern province of Szechuan is famous for its spicy cuisine, which usually features garlic, fennel, coriander and copious quantities of chilli peppers. Prawns prepared Szechuan-style are absolutely delicious; the popular smoked duck is made with ginger, cinnamon, peppercorns and orange peel.

Culinary specialities from the province of Hunan, like those of Szechuan, tend to be spicy. They include consommé with mashed pigeon, duck tongues served with mustard sauce, and fish coated with preserved fish paste.

Another highly individual cuisine comes from the region around Shanghai. It is generally more starchy than Cantonese food. The main ingredients used include salt- and freshwater fish, eels, prawns and crabs. Some dishes are flavoured with citrus fruits, especially orange and lemon. The ubiquitous sweet-and-sour fried fish originated in this region.

Drinks

The perfect compliment to Chinese food is Chinese tea, served plain in little cups. It is claimed that tea has purgative and digestive properties, which is why a small dish is always drunk before and after the meal. In most restaurants, the tea is placed automatically on every table. It is also reputedly a good solvent for fat, an important quality in view of the oily texture of some Chinese dishes. Beer is another popular accompaniment and is more palatable than than Chinese wine, which can be very sweet, or quite fiery. European and New World wines are relatively expensive in Hong Kong restaurants, but are now widely available. A fiery Chinese schnapps makes a good digestif; Maotai is the best-known example, a potent brew made of sorghum.

An alternative to tea

Food culture and etiquette

In Asia, eating is always a group activity. People enjoy going to a Chinese restaurant with a large group of friends because this provides the opportunity for boisterous conversations and the chance to order a large variety of contrasting dishes. Either the host chooses for his guests or a consensus is arrived at with a colourful parade of meat, fish and vegetable dishes, in which sweet, sour, hot, salty and bitter flavours contrast in much the same way as textures: crisp and soft, juicy and dry. All serving dishes are placed in the middle of the table and the guests simply help themselves using chopsticks. At formal banquets it is considered polite to place the choicest morsels on the guest's plate with the aid of chopsticks or a serving spoon. This procedure is repeated during each course, and toasts are exchanged several times.

If tea is being drunk, the host always tops up the cups of his guests before serving himself. The guest should

Tucking in at the Night Market

indicate his thanks by rapping lightly several times on the table with the knuckles of his right hand. This custom is based on an old story where one of the Chinese emperors, who liked to travel incognito throughout his realm, arrived at an inn accompanied by his official entourage. He courteously poured tea into the dishes of his subjects, who normally would have showed their gratitude by kowtowing to him. By doing so, however, they would have betrayed the emperor's identity. To avoid this, one of the courtiers suggested bending two fingers and rapping on the table in imitation of the kowtow, but without being noticed by onlookers.

When the teapot is empty, the lid is removed and replaced so that it only half covers the pot. The waiter or waitress will then pour fresh water onto the tea leaves. There is a story behind this practice, too. An elderly Chinese liked to spend much of his time chatting with his friends or reading in a tea house. One day, he had his pet songbird with him, and not knowing where to put it, he hid the bird in the empty teapot. A waiter came to refill the pot, but when he lifted the lid, the valuable songbird escaped. The old man sued the owner of the tea house for compensation; the latter then issued the instruction that all guests remove the lids of their teapots themselves.

By the time the plates are cleaned of the last morsel – although it is polite to leave a little to indicate the abundance of the meal – the company usually breaks up fairly quickly. It is not customary to remain seated in order to chat once the meal is over. The bill is usually settled by a single person. It would cause considerable uproar and embarrassment in any Hong Kong restaurant, irrespective of type, if one were to request separate bills. It is better to repay an invitation in kind.

Street poultry seller

Restaurant selection

It is advisable to reserve a table in advance at the more expensive restaurants, especially on Fridays, Saturdays and public holidays. Correct dress is appreciated everywhere and is essential in the top restaurants. Even in the simplest restaurants you should wait to be seated. A waiter or a special hostess will lead you to your table and hand you the menu, which in most establishments is written in Chinese and English.

The selection below represents only a fraction of what is available in Hong Kong; for further information, visitors should consult the Hong Kong Tourist Association's *Official Dining, Entertainment & Shopping Directory*, available from HKTA Visitor Information Centres.

Dried mushrooms
A practised fish cook

American Restaurant
20 Lockhart Road, Wanchai, tel: 2527 1000. Despite its name, a popular Chinese restaurant serving Peking duck.

Carrianna Chiu Chow
2/F, Hilton Tower, 95 Granville Road, Tsim Sha Tsui East, tel: 2724 4828; also at 1/F, 151 Gloucester Road, Wanchai, tel: 2511 1282. Chiu Chow cuisine with good goose and chicken dishes.

City Chiu Chow
1 and 2/F, Allied Kajima Building, 138 Gloucester Road, Wanchai, tel: 2598 4333. Specialises in seafood; recommended are oyster omelette, deep-fried crab cakes and braised squid rolls.

Dynasty
3/F, Renaissance Harbour View Hotel, 1 Harbour Road, Wanchai, tel: 2802 8888 ext. 6971 (and other locations). Opulent restaurant decorated in Tang Dynasty style, with a wide selection of Cantonese specialities.

Gaylord
1/F, Ashley Centre, 23-25 Ashley Road, Tsim Sha Tsui, tel: 2376 1001. North and South Indian cuisine with seafood and vegetarian dishes.

Hei Fung Terrace
1/F, The Repulse Bay, 109 Repulse Bay Road, Repulse Bay, tel: 2812 2622. Colourful mixture of Chinese cuisines in an elegant atmosphere in a replica of the old hotel.

House of Canton
5/F, The Lee Gardens, 33 Hysan Avenue, Causeway Bay, tel: 2907 3888. *Dim sum* at lunchtime, Cantonese specialities with a few Northern dishes at night.

Leisure: Food and Drink

Kublai's
3/F, One Capital Place, 18 Luard Road, Wanchai, tel: 2529 9117 (and other locations). Mongolian hot plate meal where guests fill their dishes at the buffet and have them cooked on hot plates in the kitchen.

Luk Yu Tea House
24–6 Stanley Street, Central, tel: 2523 5463. 1930s-style tea house famous for its delicious dim sum and somewhat surly service.

Mughal Room
1/F, Carfield Commercial Building, 75-77 Wyndham Street, Central, tel: 2524 0107. Excellent Indian restaurant; not cheap, but serving outstanding Tandoori dishes.

Al fresco dining

Nice Fragrance Vegetarian Kitchen
105–7 Thomson Road, Wanchai, tel: 2838 3067. A speciality cuisine based only on soya bean curd and vegetables. Pleasant, simple decor and friendly staff.

Peking Garden
Basement, Alexandra House, Central, tel: 2526 6465 (and other locations). Enjoyable introduction to northern Chinese cuisine, with daily noodle-making performances. Order the Beggar's Chicken and get to join in the clay-breaking ceremony.

Red Pepper
7 Lan Fong Road, Causeway Bay, tel: 2577 3811. Spicy Szechuan dishes in all variations.

Sagano
1/F, Hotel Nikko, 72 Mody Road, Tsim Sha Tsui East, tel: 2313 4215. Even here, Japanese restaurants are expensive. Sagano has a good selection of sushi and sashimi.

Shanghai Garden
Hutchison House, 10 Harcourt Road, Central, tel: 2524 8181. Shanghai cuisine with several good eel dishes, prawns and soya bean curd specialities.

Stanley's Oriental

Stanley's Oriental
90B, Stanley Main Street, Stanley, tel: 2813 9988. Pan-Asian cuisine of high quality in a renovated house on the seafront promenade at Stanley, in the south of Hong Kong Island.

Yung Kee
32-40 Wellington Street, Central, tel: 2522 1624. Traditional restaurant specialising in goose and preserved eggs.

Nightlife

Nathan Road in Kowloon

Nightclubs, bars and discos

There is a wide choice of nightclubs, from Western-style dinner-dance restaurants and casual Chinese nightclubs, to plush cabaret restaurants with floor shows. Of course there are also girlie bars where lonesome night owls can hire exotic table companions. Many of these are found in Wanchai, which has failed to shake off its 'Suzie Wong' image, although there are a number of ordinary restaurants and bars, particularly in Lockhart Road.

Many of the more expensive hostess clubs are to be found in a forest of flashing neon signs in Tsim Sha Tsui East. They feature plush décor, excellent music and a wide choice of international hostesses.

The younger set mostly heads for the bars and clubs of Lan Kwai Fong and SoHo (South of Hollywood Road) above the Central district. Tsim Sha Tsui also has quite a selection of bars and pubs, many of them in Ashley Road or the side streets off Carnarvon Road, such as Knutsford Terrace. If you want to play it safe, head for one of the bars and discotheques in the larger hotels, which tend to be packed on Friday, Saturday and the eves of public holidays, when premium charges apply. The action usually doesn't start until around 10pm and continues well into the small hours. Hong Kong's top nightclubs are JJs at the Grand Hyatt Hotel and Manhattan Westworld in the Renaissance Harbour View Hotel.

Night lights in Jordan Road

Food first

Before setting out to paint the town red, however, you should ensure your tanks are well filled. For the Chinese this means a generous dinner with as many companions as possible. Many visitors will prefer to pick a restaurant for its view rather than its food. Some afford a spectacular view of the harbour, or the South China Sea, for example the Verandah at Repulse Bay or eateries along Stanley Main Street. You could also take the ferry to Lamma or Cheung Chau and select your supper from the fish swimming in tanks in the seafood restaurants by the harbour. On clear nights, take in the breathtaking panorama from The Peak, where Café Deco and the Peak Café are the best bets. It's a good idea to reserve a table. Harbour tours are also on offer with meals included at the kitschy but memorable Jumbo Floating Restaurant in Aberdeen

On the Waterfront Promenade

Bright lights

For a constantly changing view of Hong Kong's bright lights, get on a tram in Central and travel to Causeway Bay. It is one of the cheapest nocturnal pleasures in town. Arriving at your destination you can spend some of the money you've saved in the shops.

You could also go to the famous Night Market on Temple Street north of Kowloon Park, at its liveliest from 7pm–10pm. Follow this with a leisurely stroll along the Kowloon Waterfront Promenade, the lights of Hong Kong island providing a breathtaking nighttime panorama.

Horse racing

During the winter months, from September to May, there is horse racing twice a week in Happy Valley and Sha Tin. It's a worthwhile pastime even if you don't intend to risk a few dollars on a bet, but prefer to watch the experts and soak up the atmosphere on the vast stands

Cinema

Hong Kong is a film-makers' city. Its wide range of cinemas offer an international repertory, with an emphasis on the latest Hollywood blockbusters (English with Chinese subtitles) and locally-produced action movies (Chinese with English subtitles). For art-house movies, try the Hong Kong Arts Centre, Cine Arts or Broadway Cinematheque.

Classical culture

With so many modern distractions, classical culture tends to take second place. Despite earnest efforts on the part of the government and other bodies, except for the festival weeks Hong Kong has never become a cultural mecca. Nonetheless, there are performances by the Hong Kong Ballet, and the Hong Kong Chinese and Philharmonic Orchestras with guest peformances by visiting stars. Local repertory groups put on regular theatre productions either in English or Cantonese. The daily newspapers and free listings magazines publish a calendar of events, brochures are available at City Hall and in the Arts Centre, and hotel concierges are a mine of local information.

Shopping and Markets

Indian tailors display their wares

With an almost endless array of goods available, Hong Kong continues to be a shopping paradise. But it has long ceased to be a bargain, particularly for electronics, where inflation and exorbitant rents have pared down the difference between local and European prices. Be wary of confidence tricksters who sell fake goods in original packages. It is essential to check prices at home, and to obtain an international guarantee. Highly recommended are member outlets of the Hong Kong Tourist Association (HKTA); they can be recognised by the sign on the door, red circle logo showing a red junk on a white background. A list of these outlets is contained in the HKTA's free *Official Dining, Entertainment & Shopping Guide*.

The clothing on offer in the city's countless designer boutiques is also not much cheaper than in Europe or the United States, although there is a wide range of cheap merchandise available in the shops and markets, e.g. in Temple Street and in Stanley. Made-to-measure clothing is good value, provided the tailor has sufficient time to do a good job. Two fittings are necessary for a suit if it is to fit properly. Watches and jewellery are available in vast profusion. Here, too, a receipt is essential. The price of gold varies according to the current market value, and the amount of gold in an item of jewellery must be precisely stated. Jade is a green or white precious stone much loved by the Chinese. When choosing jade, make sure that the stone has a translucent lustre to it: avoid stones that have a milky appearance. If you plan to invest large sums, it is advisable to take along an expert.

The same applies to antiques, which are offered for sale mainly in Hollywood Road above the Central district. Prices are high and there are many fakes, some of them sold with certificates of authenticity.

Watches galore

Hollywood Road antique store

Depending on their origins, Hong Kong's department stores stock a varying range of goods. The mainland Chinese department store chains offer goods from all over China. These days, international manufacturers produce many items, including clothing, shoes, toys and suitcases, in China, and you will find brands meant for export selling in Hong Kong. Japanese department stores tend to cater to the luxury market and offer goods from all over the world. Lane Crawford, the oldest and one of the most prestigious department stores in Hong Kong, can look back on many years of colonial history. Today, it is largely a series of boutiques, specialising in high-end fashions, accessories and luxury household goods.

Expensive home furnishings and accessories are sold at shops that import their goods from Europe's leading manufacturers. Carpets from China, Tibet, Pakistan, Afghanistan and India are available in abundance. Inexpensive sports equipment is also widely available.

Although department stores and many shops have fixed prices, bargaining is an almost essential part of the game elsewhere. You usually get a better deal if you pay cash, but don't expect huge discounts, as prices tend to be fairly rigid. It is better to compare prices in one district with another rather than between shops on the same street.

Carpet sellers

Souvenir mask

Shopping centres

Harbour City (Ocean Terminal, Ocean Centre, Ocean Galleries and The Gateway), 3–27 Canton Road, Tsim Sha Tsui. Interconnecting malls offering acres of boutiques and shops, mostly selling clothing and shoes.

The Landmark, 16 Des Voeux Road, Central. Exclusive boutiques in a building with a large atrium.

Pacific Place, 88 Queensway, Admiralty. Spacious shopping, cinema, hotel and restaurant complex on the boundary between Central and Wanchai.

Chinese department stores

Chinese Arts & Crafts (HK) Ltd, China Resources Building, 26 Harbour Road, Wanchai; Shop 230 Pacific Place, 88 Queensway; Star House, 3 Salisbury Road, Tsim Sha Tsui; Nathan Hotel, 378 Nathan Road, Jordan. A wide range of items produced in China.

CRC Department Store Ltd, 92–104 Queen's Road Central; 31 Yee Wo Street, Causeway Bay; 65 Argyle Street, Mong Kok. Less expensive Chinese chain.

Hong Kong department stores

Lane Crawford, 70 Queen's Road Central; Pacific Place, 88 Queensway; Times Square, Causeway Bay; Shop 100 Ocean Terminal, Harbour City, Tsim Sha Tsui. Long-established store with a wide range of goods.

Jewellery display

Shanghai Tang, Pedder Building, 8 Theatre Lane, Central. Stylish reinterpretations of traditional Chinese clothes (off-the-peg and custom-tailored).

Japanese department stores
Mitsukoshi, 500 Hennessy Road, Causeway Bay; Sun Plaza, 28 Canton Road, Tsim Sha Tsui. Exclusive selection of goods in a series of boutiques; lovely porcelain.
Seibu, Pacific Place, 88 Queensway, Admiralty. The best of the best, from antique furniture to French artichokes.
Sogo, 555 Hennessy Road, Causeway Bay. An entire floor of perfumes, several floors of women's and men's clothing plus a wide range of sports items.

Tailors
Pacific Custom Tailors, 322 Pacific Place, 88 Queensway, Central.
Tailor Kwan (Creative Tailoring) Central Escalator Link Alley, 2/F Central Market.
Yuen's Tailors, Central Escalator Link Alley, 2/F Central Market.
Y. William Yu, 46 Mody Road, Tsim Sha Tsui.

Street stalls and lanes
Sheung Wan: the Hollywood Road/Upper Lascar Row (Cat Street) area offers everything from antique works of art, porcelain and furniture, to modern reproductions. Man Wa Lane for traditional Chinese chops (seals) in jade, bone and hard stone; Western Market for a wide range of fabrics and handicrafts from all over the world.
Central: Li Yuen Street East and Li Yuen Streets East & West ('the lanes') for inexpensive clothes, handbags, costume jewellery and household goods in a true bazaar atmosphere; Theatre Lane for shoeshine services and repairs, locksmiths and engravers; Pottinger Street for haberdashery, brushes, combs and hair ornaments, etc.
Causeway Bay: Jardine's Crescent for garments, accessories and household goods in a real street market, and Jardine's Bazaar for dried foods, bean curd (tofu), etc.
Kowloon: the Ladies' Market in Tung Choi Street in Mong Kok for inexpensive women's clothes and accessories; the Jade Market in Kansu Street, Yau Ma Tei, open daily 10am–3.30pm; Temple Street Night Market for sweaters, shirts, gadgets, CDs and more; best visited after 7pm.

Factory outlets
Located in all major shopping areas but mainly in Central District, Cameron Road in Tsim Sha Tsui and Hung Hom (Kowloon). A wide range of export garments including designer items. The HKTA publishes a list of recommended outlets, free from Visitor Information Centres.

Tea ware

Getting There

Opposite: chop carvers await your custom

By air

Hong Kong is served by dozens of airlines, including its flagship carrier Cathay Pacific, and the world's biggest airport terminal. Opened in 1998, Hong Kong International Airport is a state-of-the-art facility located at Chek Lap Kok off the north shore of Lantau Island. While there may be some who miss the heart-stopping final approach through high-rises to the old airport at Kai Tak, Chek Lap Kok's light and airy glass structure with its aerodynamically curving roof, set against the backdrop of Lantau's mountains, has won many fans.

Curves at Chek Lap Kok

The fastest way to get to and from Chek Lap Kok is by the high-speed Airport Express Line (AEL) railway, which links the airport to Hong Kong Station in Central in just 23 minutes, with stops at Tsing Yi and Kowloon Station near Tsim Sha Tsui. Tickets to and from Hong Kong Station cost HK$70 for single/day return; HK$120 for a return ticket valid for one month; to and from Kowloon Station HK$60 and HK$100, respectively. Trains depart every 10 minutes from 6am–1am daily. Airport Express passengers can take free shuttle bus transfers between the Hong Kong and Kowloon Stations to 21 major hotels, the KCR station at Hung Hom and the China Ferry Terminal. MTR underground railway connections at Tsing Yi and Hong Kong Station provide access to other areas of Hong Kong and Kowloon.

A cheaper but slower alternative is to take the MTR line to Tung Chung (HK$23) and a shuttle bus to the airport.

If you prefer to travel by bus, there are eight Airbus and 22 conventional franchised bus routes to choose from. Average journey time is about one hour and tickets vary from HK$20 to HK$45. Bus services operate around-the-clock.

Taxis are readily available in either direction. At the airport taxi pick-up area, they are zoned according to the area they serve (red for urban Kowloon and Hong Kong; green for the New Territories and blue for Lantau Island). Approximate costs in each direction are HK$330 for Central and HK$270 for Tsim Sha Tsui, including bridge and tunnel fees.

By sea

Hong Kong is one of the cruising hubs of Asia. Over 60 international cruise ships berth beside Ocean Terminal wharf in Tsim Sha Tsui each year. At the top end of the line, it is a port of call on Round the World and Exotic East tours for such famous cruise ships as Cunard's *Queen Elizabeth II* (QE2) and Royal Viking Sun, Holland America Westours' *Nieuw Amsterdam* and Radisson Seven Seas' *Song of Flower*.

The luxury way to go

Getting Around

Hong Kong has a remarkable range of public transport facilities which are both efficient and inexpensive. Some can even claim to be amongst the city's most famous sights.

Mass Transit Railway (MTR)

This underground railway network runs along four interconnecting lines serving the north side of Hong Kong Island, Kowloon, the southern fringe of the New Territories, Tsing Yi and Tung Chung on Lantau Island. The MTR connects with the high-speed Airport Express Line at Hong Kong Station and Tsing Yi; and with the KCR overland railway at Kowloon Tong. The cost depends on the route taken. Purchase your ticket before passing through the turnstiles; the automatic ticket machines accept HK$10

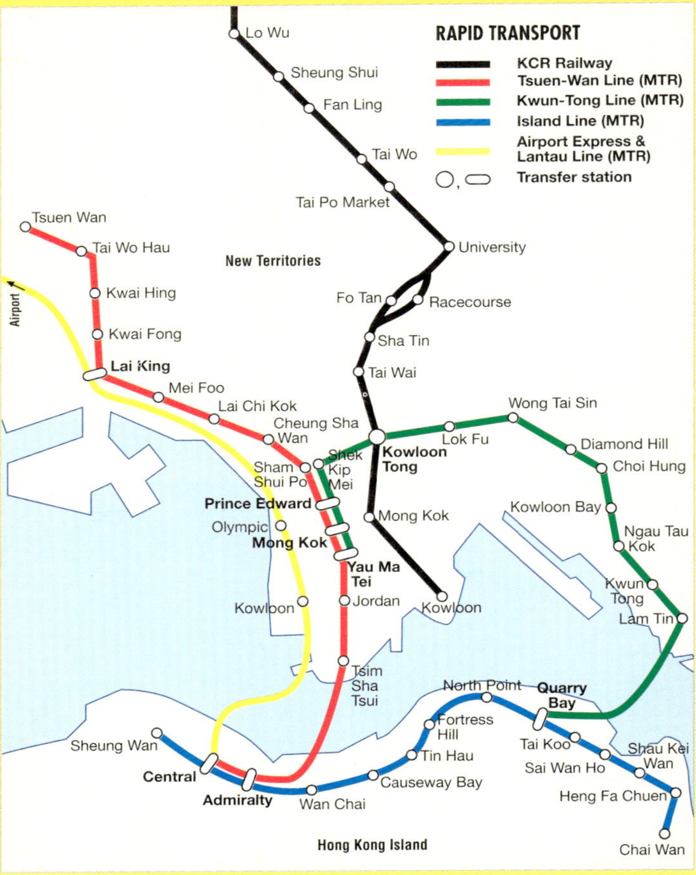

The MTR is clean and efficient

coins down to 50 cent coins. Adult single fares range from HK$4 to HK$26. Individual tickets are only valid for the day of issue. Visitors staying more than a few days might find it worthwhile to buy an Octopus stored-value card which allows you to travel on the Airport Express, MTR, KCR, LRT and some buses and ferries at slightly lower fares. Octopus cards can be purchased at customer service counters at Airport Express and MTR stations. The minimum price is HK$150 which includes a HK$50 deposit (refundable from Airport Express and MTR station customer service counters).

Kowloon-Canton Railway (KCR)

The KCR logo

This overland railway runs between Hung Hom, Mong Kok and Kowloon Tong stations in Kowloon and the border station at Lo Wu. The intermediate stations provide convenient access to the towns and villages of the New Territories; the farthest you can go without a China visa is Sheung Shui. The KCR is great value. Unless you are travelling on into China, the maximum fare (Hung Hom to Sheung Shui) is HK$9 (ordinary class) or HK$18 (first class). It costs slightly less if you use an Octopus stored-value card (see MTR).

Light Rail Transit (LRT)

The LRT serves the western New Territories

This is a high-speed overland railway running between Tuen Mun ferry pier and Yuen Long in the western New Territories. Trains run from 5.40am to 12.30am daily. Fares start at HK$4.

Tram

The tram is the ideal means of transport for short trips along the north coast of Hong Kong Island or for a leisurely outing, especially at night, through the streets of Wanchai and Causeway Bay. The entrance is at the rear, and you should give yourself ample time to get to the exit at the front, where you drop HK$2 (HK$1 for under 12s) into the fare box next to the driver as you leave.

Peak Tram

For more than a century the Peak Tram (which is really a funicular railway) has provided the quickest way of ascending The Peak. The tram takes only 7–8 minutes to cover the 0.9-mile (1.4-km) route whilst ascending to 1,174ft (367m). For the best views, get a window seat on the right side on your way up and on the left side on the way down. The tram runs approximately every 10 minutes until midnight. Adults HK$18 (single), HK$28 (return); under 12s HK$5 (single), HK$8 return. There is a free open-top shuttle bus from the Star Ferry concourse in Central to the lower terminus on Garden Road.

Buses are cheap

Buses
Double-decker buses, which run from 6am till midnight, cover most parts of the territory. Fares range from HK$1.20 for short journeys in the city to HK$45 for longer trips into the New Territories. You drop the fare into a box as you enter and no change is given so it's a good idea to keep plenty of small change handy. Some buses also accept Octopus stored-value cards (see MTR).

Minibuses
Yellow with a red stripe, these cover fixed routes, although they stop anywhere to pick up passengers, who indicate that they wish to embark by holding out their arm. To disembark, one simply shouts. The fare is listed on a table, or the driver simply announces the cost when one disembarks. Fares range from HK$2 to HK$20.

Maxicabs
Yellow with a green stripe, these run along specific routes and have fixed prices ranging from HK$1.50 to HK$18. A sign on the front indicates the destination.

Ferries
No trip to Hong Kong is complete without a trip across the harbour on the Star Ferry. In operation since 1898, it links the tip of Tsim Sha Tsui with Central District and covers a second route to Wanchai. At HK$2.20 (upper deck) and HK$1.70 (lower deck), it must be one of the cheapest and most scenic ferry rides in the world. Fares are paid at the automatic turnstiles at the entrance. The service runs from 6.30am–11.30pm and the crossing takes 8 minutes.

Passenger ferries also run to the Outlying Islands (Cheung Chau, Lamma, Lantau and Peng Chau), Tsing Yi and Tsuen Wan from the Central Ferry Piers in front of Exchange Square and Hong Kong Station (to the west of the Star Ferry Concourse in Central). Ferries to Cheung Chau leave from Pier 6 and ferries to Lantau (Mui Wo) and Peng Chau leave from Pier 7. Ferries to Lamma, Tsing Yi and Tsuen Wan leave from Pier 5. Fares range from HK$10 on weekdays to HK$30 for a Sunday/holiday crossing on a fast ferry.

Inner city cabs

Taxi
Hong Kong taxis have signs on the roof and a red plate proclaiming 'For Hire' on the windscreen. In the inner city they are red with silver roofs, in the New Territories, green with white roofs and on Lantau they are blue with white roofs. There are extra charges for tunnel tolls, booked calls, luggage stored in the trunk/boot and luggage handling. Receipts are available on request. New Territories and Lantau taxis charge slightly lower fares.

Discussing itineraries

Facts for the Visitor

Visas
Most visitors only need a valid passport to enter Hong Kong. The length of visa-free tourist visit allowed varies according to nationality. British subjects holding full UK passports are granted six months upon entry. All other European Union nationals get three months, as do nationals of Australia and the US.

Customs
Hong Kong remains a free port, and taxes are levied only on alcohol, tobacco and perfume. The tax-free allowances are one litre wine or spirits, 200 cigarettes or 250g tobacco, and 60ml perfume. If you carry firearms, they must be declared and handed over for safe-keeping until you depart. There are also stringent restrictions on the import and export of ivory and other items from endangered species protected by CITES (Convention on International Trade in Endangered Species of Wild Fauna and Flora).

Tourist information
The Hong Kong Tourist Association (HKTA) is the official body representing the tourism industry in Hong Kong.
In the UK: 6 Grafton Street, London W1X 3LB, tel: 0171-533 7100.
In the US: 5th Floor, 590 Fifth Avenue, New York, NY 10036-4706, tel: 212-869 5008/9; Suite 1220, 10940 Wilshire Boulevard, Los Angeles, CA 90024-3915, tel: 310-208 4582; 401 N. Michigan Avenue, Suite #1640, Chicago, IL, tel: 313-329 1828.
In Hong Kong: HKTA operates a multilingual Visitor Hotline, tel: 2508 1234; and two Visitor Information Centres in town at the Star Ferry Concourse, Tsim Sha Tsui

(Monday to Friday 8am–6pm; weekends and public holidays 8am–6pm) and Shop 8, Basement, Jardine House, Central (Monday to Friday 9am–6pm; Saturday 9am–1pm; closed Sunday and public holidays). There is also a Visitor Information Centre at Hong Kong International Airport (daily 6am–midnight).

Sightseeing tours

The HKTA organises special tours and programmes on a regular basis. These include 'The Land Between' Tour, Sports and Recreation Tour, Come Horseracing Tour, Heritage Tours and Family Insight Tour. Brochures are available at the Visitor Information Centres.

Gray Line Tours of HK Ltd (2368 7111) and Watertours of HK Ltd (tel: 2739 3302) offer a variety of water and/or land tours, some including lunch or dinner; and MP Tours Ltd (tel: 2118 6243) offer Star Ferry cruises around Victoria Harbour and Open-top Tram Tours on vintage trams.

See the endangered dolphins

Chinese pleasure junk

Hong Kong Dolphinwatch (tel: 2982 1414) offer regular boat trips through the scenic western harbour to the swimming grounds of the endangered Chinese White Dolphin (Sousa chinensis). You can also charter a 53-ft Chinese pleasure junk complete with 2 crew members from Simpson Marine in Aberdeen (tel: 2555 7349).

Currency and exchange

The local currency is the Hong Kong Dollar (HK$) which is pegged loosely to the US Dollar at an approximate rate of US$1 to HK$7.80. Banknotes are issued by three banks and have different motifs but similar colours. They are available in the following denominations: HK$ 1,000, 500, 100, 50, 20 and 10. Coins are available to the value of HK$ 10, 5, 2 and 1 as well as 50, 20 and 10 cents.

Credit cards are widely accepted, and there are large numbers of cash dispensers. American Express cardholders have access to Jetco automatic teller machines (ATMs) and can withdraw local currency and cash traveller's cheques at Express Cash ATMs. Holders of Visa and MasterCard can also obtain local currency from the Hongkong Bank (HSBC) and Hang Seng Bank ATMs.

Banks, licensed money changers and hotels will exchange cash and encash traveller's cheques. Banks charge commission up to HK$30 for cash exchanges, and HK$50 for traveller's cheques. Hotels and money changers charge no commission but offer less favourable exchange rates. Traveller's cheques can be encashed free of charge by the issuing company: American Express, 1/F, Henley Building, 5 Queen's Road Central; Thomas Cook, 18/F, Vicwood Plaza, 199 Des Voeux Road Central.

Major banks are open Monday to Friday 9am–4.30pm, Saturday 9am–12.30pm.

Tipping

Tipping is always welcomed. Most restaurants add a 10 percent service charge to the bill; if the service is particularly good, guests should leave a few coins or – in the case of larger bills, a few notes – on the table. Where no service charge has been added to the bill, it is customary to tip 10 percent (or more).

The hotel porters who carry your luggage usually expect to receive about HK$10–20, and in top hotels even more. The friendly attendants in the washrooms normally receive HK$2–5.

Local people seldom tip taxi drivers, but, like taxi drivers all over the world, they will be very glad if you do give them something extra.

Souvenirs

Hong Kong is a shopping paradise in which there is almost nothing money cannot buy. This means that there are also items here which travellers should refrain from purchasing. In Hong Kong, this applies in particular to ivory and products derived from endangered species, such as tigers and rhinoceroses, which are (in theory) protected by CITES (see Customs) but are unfortunately revered in Chinese lore for their aphrodisiac properties.

Shop opening times

There are no legal restrictions; the following times may be taken as a guide:
Tsim Sha Tsui, Yaumatei, Mongkok: 10am–9pm
Tsim Sha Tsui East: 10am–7.30pm
Central: 10am–6pm; many shops closed on Sunday
Wanchai, Causeway Bay: 10am–9.30pm

Postal services

The main post offices are next to the Star Ferry in Central and at 10 Middle Road, Tsim Sha Tsui. Both are open from Monday to Saturday 8am to 6pm; Sunday and some public holidays 8am to 2pm. The numerous branch post offices throughout the territory have shorter opening hours and are closed on Sunday, public holidays and Saturday afternoon. Hotels usually sell postage stamps and will mail guests' post if requested.

Characteristic mail boxes

Telephone

In principle, local calls in Hong Kong are free. In practice, most public places have payphones and local calls cost HK$1. You can make standard international direct dial (IDD) calls from public card phones with a stored-value phone card (HK$50 to HK$300; available at HKTA Visitor Information Centres, 7-Eleven stores and some bookshops). You can also make IDD calls from sound-proof

Keeping up communications

booths and send faxes at the following Cable and Wireless HKT shops: 161 Des Voeux Road, Central. Tel: 2534 0603; 147 Johnston Road, Wan Chai. Tel: 2892 1997; Basement, London Plaza, 219 Nathan Road, Jordan. Tel: 2710 6633 (open 10 am to 7 pm Monday to Saturday; closed Sunday and holidays); and Ground Floor, Hermes House, 10 Middle Road, Tsim Sha Tsui. Tel: 2724 8322/2888 7185 (24 hours daily). The service centres operate on a cash or stored-value phonecard basis only; credit cards and cheques are not accepted. Note that many hotels charge a 'handling fee' on local and IDD calls.

International dialling codes: to Hong Kong: 852 (no additional code is required for subscribers within the city limits); from Hong Kong, dial 001 (telephone) or 002 (fax), followed by the country code, the exchange code (without the zero) and finally the subscriber's number.

Time
Hong Kong time is GMT plus 8 hours.

Voltage
The voltage is 220V/50Hz. However, three-pin plugs of various sizes and shapes are required to fit the sockets. Adaptors are available in hotels and supermarkets, and at better hotels you will find sockets for electric shavers and built-in hair driers.

Units of measurement
Hong Kong is gradually going metric. However, property is still measured in square feet and beer in pints; while traditional Chinese measures such as the catty (about 1.5lbs or 670 grams) are still used in fresh food markets and gold is sold by the tael (about 1.3 ounces or 38 grams).

Disabled visitors
With the exception of Hong Kong International Airport, major hotels and some of the newer public and commercial buildings, Hong Kong is not an easy place for disabled visitors to navigate. Two useful publications to consult are HKTA's free Access Guide for Disabled Visitors (available from HKTA Visitor Information Centres) and the Transport Department's Guide to Public Transport Services in Hong Kong for Disabled Persons (available from the Transport Department, 41st Floor, Immigration Tower, Gloucester Road, Wan Chai; tel: 2829 5223).

Public holidays
The most important Western, Christian, Chinese and religious festivals are all observed. Most shops remain open for at least half a day on these special days, except during Chinese New Year. Traditional Chinese festivals are based

on the lunar calendar and therefore vary from year to year. (If a festival falls on a Sunday or two festivals coincide, the day preceding or following the festival is usually designated as a general holiday.)
New Year's Day: January 1
Lunar New Year: three days in late January/February
Good Friday: March or April
Saturday following Good Friday: March or April
Easter Monday: March or April
Ching Ming Festival: April
Labour Day: May 1
Buddha's Birthday: May
Tuen Ng (Dragon Boat) Festival: June
Hong Kong Special Administrative Region Establishment Day: July 1
Day following Mid-Autumn Festival: September
China National Day: October 1
Chung Yeung Festival: October
Christmas Day: December 25
First weekday after Christmas Day: December

Television

There are two English-language terrestrial channels. Programmes include a selection of locally produced shows as well as features from the UK, the United States and Australia. Most hotels also subscribe to the satellite Star TV and/or Cable TV.

Radio

Six English-language channels provide a wide range of programmes. The BBC World Service is relayed around the clock via RTHK Radio 6 on 675 kHz.

Newspapers

The two local English-language daily newspapers are the South China Morning Post and the Hong Kong Standard. Apart from daily news, you will also find information about cultural events, cinema programmes and on Wednesday (during the racing season) a supplement devoted to horse racing. The free entertainment listings magazines, HK Magazine (weekly) and BC Magazine (monthly), are also useful for finding out what's going on.

Photography

Apart from camps and military complexes there are no restrictions on photography. Nonetheless, photographers should bear in mind the rights of the individual to his or her privacy. Always negotiate a poser's fee before taking photos of the rickshaw drivers at the Star Ferry Concourse in Central or the Hakka women in the New Territories.

Dress

Loose-fitting light clothing made of natural fibres is suitable almost all the year round. Revealing attire and casual sports gear are not appreciated by the local residents except in the appropriate places. For all business encounters, exercise prudence and dress conservatively. The same applies in many restaurants at night.

Health precautions

No vaccinations are required to enter Hong Kong. During the past few years there have been a number of cases of Hepatitis A and food poisoning, caused by insufficiently cooked fish and seafood from the heavily polluted Hong Kong coastal waters or by green leafy vegetables from China which had been contaminated by pesticides. It is advisable to exercise caution when eating from street stalls. If you are especially worried about food hygiene, you can always stick to hotels and smarter restaurants, many of which import jet-fresh ingredients from Australasia, the States or Europe.

The excessively cool temperatures in air-conditioned buildings may lead to a chill when the weather is hot and humid outside. A jacket or pullover affords protection. A sunhat and suntan lotion are necessary for extended periods outdoors. You'll need mosquito repellent after dusk in rural areas.

Medical

Most hospitals offer services to a high medical standard. The doctors are trained in Western or Chinese medicine and usually speak English as they have studied abroad. Treatment must be paid for in cash; check with your health insurance company beforehand concerning the procedure for claiming reimbursement. Medicines are widely available. Doctors often sell the necessary medicines in their clinics; chemist's shops are also well stocked. For the sake of convenience, travellers should bring adequate supplies of commonly used medicines.

Hotels will assist if you need a doctor in an emergency. For ambulance service in Kowloon, tel: 2713 5555; on Hong Kong Island, tel: 2576 6555; tel: 2639 2555 in the New Territories.

Ready to assist

Emergencies

Police, Fire, Ambulance, tel: 999

Diplomatic representation

British Consulate General, 1 Supreme Court Road, Admiralty, tel: 2901 3000/3111.
Consulate of the United States of America, 26 Garden Road, Central, Hong Kong, tel: 2523 9011.

Accommodation

The lobby of the Grand Hyatt

Hong Kong has more than a hundred hotels of international standard, and virtually all the larger groups and chains have at least one establishment here.

Hong Kong's most expensive hotels such as the Mandarin, Peninsula, Regent Hong Kong, Grand Hyatt and Island Shangri-La cluster around the Tsim Sha Tsui waterfront on Kowloon-side; the HK Convention and Exhibition Centre in Wanchai; Pacific Place in Admiralty; and Statue Square/Chater Gardens in Central. These luxury establishments are continually voted among the best in the world in terms of service, facilities and cuisine; and charge upwards of HK$2,500 a night.

Many tourists (and tour group operators) prefer the hotels around Nathan and Canton Roads in Tsim Sha Tsui or Causeway Bay on Hong Kong Island, both lively areas offering good transport and great shopping and dining choices. The hotels further up Nathan Road, in Yau Ma Tei and Mong Kok, and older parts of Wanchai tend to be smaller and cheaper.

Many Hong Kong hotels offer 'value-added' packages or discounts (of up to 60 percent in some cases) on published 'rack' rates. It's definitely worth doing some advance research through travel agents, the HKTA or the Internet; as well as looking into combined air ticket and accommodation packages.

Alternatives to city-centre accommodation include the luxury Gold Coast Resort in the New Territories and the enormous, new Regal Airport Hotel at Chek Lap Kok. There are also a handful of small, no-frills establishments on the islands of Cheung Chau, Lamma and Lantau, and out at Sai Kung. A yet more rural and spartan (but very cheap) alternative are the seven youth hostels run by the Hong Kong Youth Hostel Association (tel: 2788 1638).

Hotel selection

BP International House, 8 Austin Road, Jordan, tel: 2376 1111; fax: 2376 1333. Plain but comfortable rooms beside Kowloon Park. Good value.

Caritas Bianchi Lodge, 4 Cliff Road, Yau Ma Tei, tel: 2388 1111; fax: 2770 6669. Clean, spacious rooms in well-run Catholic hostel. Good value.

Century Harbour Hotel, 508 Queen's Road West, Western, tel: 2974 1234, fax: 2213 6642. New hotel in the heart of the traditional Western district. Good value.

Century Hong Kong Hotel, 238 Jaffe Road, Wanchai, tel: 2598 8888; fax: 2598 8866. Not luxurious, but in the heart of Wanchai.

Excelsior, 281 Gloucester Road, Causeway Bay, tel: 2894 8888; fax: 2895 6459. Well-run, compact hotel overlooking Victoria Harbour and the colourful Causeway Bay typhoon shelter.

Hotel Furama Hong Kong, 1 Connaught Road, Central, tel: 2525 5111; fax: 2845 9339. Quietly plush business hotel. Convenient location in Central.

Holiday Inn Golden Mile, 50 Nathan Road, Tsim Sha Tsui, tel: 2369 3111; fax: 2369 8016. Popular hotel along Kowloon's main shopping thoroughfare.

Hyatt Regency, 67 Nathan Road, Tsim Sha Tsui, tel: 2311 1234; fax: 2739 8701. Upper-category hotel along the Nathan Road shopping thoroughfare.

Sign of elegance

Island Shangri-La Hong Kong, 88 Queensway, Central, tel: 2877 3838; fax: 2521 8742. The flagship of the Shangri-La group with elegant furnishings and pleasant service. Above the Pacific Place shopping complex.

Regal Airport Hotel, 9 Cheong Tat Road, Chek Lap Kok, tel: 2286 8888; fax: 2286 8686. Hong Kong's largest hotel tucked in beside the world's largest airport.

The Emperor (Happy Valley) Hotel, 1A Wang Tak Street, Happy Valley, tel: 2893 3693, fax: 2834 6777. Boutique hotel in peaceful location near Happy Valley racecourse, only minutes away from Causeway Bay.

The Park Lane, 310 Gloucester Road, Causeway Bay, tel: 2890 3355; fax: 2890 3620. Relaxing view across Victoria Park in this attractive, well-run hotel.

The Peninsula, Salisbury Road, Tsim Sha Tsui, tel: 2366 6251; fax: 2722 4170. This epitome of colonial hotels has given in to high-tech creature comforts with its 30-storey extension. The lobby still boasts golden chandeliers.

The Royal Pacific Hotel and Towers, 33 Canton Road, Tsim Sha Tsui, tel: 2738 2222; fax: 2736 5119. Excellent value for money above the shopping paradise of Ocean Centre.

The Salisbury (YMCA), 41 Salisbury Road, Tsim Sha Tsui, tel: 2369 2211; fax: 2739 9315. Well-appointed YMCA next door to the Peninsula. Great value.

Index

Aberdeen......................34
Aberdeen Harbour.......34
Altar to the
 Earth Deity,
 Cheung Chau......**59–60**
Amah (Mother)
 Rock.........................**45**

Bank of China.............24
Botanical and
 Zoological Gardens ..26
bronze Buddha........**56–7**
Bonham Strand West ..20
Bun Festival................**59**

Cafe Deco 33
Cat Street......................17
Causeway Bay..............30
Cenotaph 24
Central District........**22–6**
Central Market 16
Central Plaza 28
Cheung Chau.........**58–61**
Cheung Sha 54
Chi Ma Wan
 Peninsula 54
Chinese University
 Art Museum..............47
Ching Chung
 Koon Temple............50
Ching Ming..................**68**
chop carvers 21
City Festival.................**69**
City Hall.......................22
Clock Tower.................38
Confucianism **63–4**
Cultural Centre............38

D'Aguilar
 Peninsula 37
Deep Water Bay..........35
Dim Sum.....................**71**
Dragon Boat
 Festival.....................**68**

Eastern New
 Territories.............**44–7**
Exchange Square.........23

Film Festival **69**
Flagstaff House (see
 Museum of Tea Ware)

Government House.....25

Happy Valley..............29
Harbour City 41
Hau Wong Temple......55
HK. Arts Centre 28
Hollywood Road 17
Hollywood Park 18
Hong Kong Academy
 for Performing Arts ..28
Hong Kong Arts
 Festival.....................**69**
Hong Kong Club.........24
Hong Kong
 Convention and
 Exhibition Centre...28
Hong Kong Island.**16–37**
Hong Kong Museum
 of Art **39**
Hong Kong Park 26
Hongkong and
 Shanghai Bank..........25
Hopewell Centre 27
Hung Shing
 Temple..................**50–1**
Hung Shing Ye
 Beach........................**61**

Jade Market 41
Jardine Bazaar.............30
Jardine Crescent..........30
Jardine House..............23
Jumbo Floating
 Restaurant.................35

Kowloon **38–43**
Kowloon Mosque........40
Kowloon Park 40
Kun Ting Study Hall...51
Kwan Tai Temple........55
Kwun Yam Wan
 Beach........................**60**

Ladder Street...............17
Ladies' Market 41
Lamma **61**
Landmark, The 23
Lantau Island...........**53–7**
Lantern Festival **67–8**
Legislative Council
 Building....................24
Lei Cheng Uk, ...**48–9**
Lion Rock....................**45**
Lippo Centre 27
Lucky numbers............**66**
Lugard Road................33

Man Mo Temple,
 (Tai Po) **47**
Man Mo Temple,
 (Hollywood Road)....17
Mandarin Oriental
 Hotel.........................**23**
Middle Kingdom.........35
Miu Fat Temple...........**50**
Mid-Autumn Festival..**68**
Mui Wo **53**
Museum of History 40
Museum of
 Tea Ware 26

Nathan Road...**38**, **39–40**
New Territories **44–52**
Night Market
 (Temple St.) **43**
Noonday Gun **30–1**

Ocean Centre 41
Ocean Park 35
Ocean Terminal 41
Outlying Districts
 Pier **58**, **61**

Pacific Place 27
Pak She Praya Road....**58**
Pak Tai Temple **58–9**
Peak Cafe 33
Peak Galleria...............33
Peak Tram 26, **32–3**
Peak, The.................**32–3**
Peninsula Hotel...........41
Ping Shan
 Heritage Trail **50**
Po Fook
 Ancestry Hall............**46**
Po Lin Monastery........**56**
Possession Street.........18
Prince's Building 23
Pui O **53**

Queen's Pier 22
Queen's Road East......27
Queen's Road West.....19

Railway Museum........**47**
Repulse Bay 35

Sai Wan Pier...............**61**
Sam Tung Uk **49**
Sha Tin **47**
Sha Tin Racecourse....**47**
Shek O Country
 Park..........................37
Sheung Cheung Wai ...**51**
Silvermine Bay
 (see *Mui Wo*) **53**
Sok Kwu Wan **61**
Space Museum............**39**
St John's
 Cathedral 25
Standard Chartered
 Bank 25
Stanley.........................36
Stanley Market............36
Star Ferry Pier 22
Statue Square 24
Sunset Peak **53**

Tai Fu Tai....................**52**
Tai O **54–6**
Tai Po Market **47**
Taoism.....................**64–6**
Tang Family
 Ancestral Halls **51**
Tea Plantation **57**
Temple Street..............**43**
Ten Thousand
 Buddhas Monastery
 (Man Fat Tze) ...**46–7**
Tin Hau
 temples ...**31**, 34, **36**, **42**
Tsui Shing Lau
 Pagoda **52**
Tuen Mun....................**49**
Tung Chung Fort.........**57**
Tung Wan Beach **60**

Victoria Park...............**31**

Wanchai **27–9**
Wanchai Post
 Office........................28
Waterfront Promenade
 (Kowloon) **39**
Western District ...**16–21**
Western Market...........20
Western New
 Territories **48–52**
Wong Tai Sin
 Temple..................**44–5**

Yeung Hau Temple.....**51**
Yuen Po Street
 Bird Garden 41
Yung Shue Wan **61**

© APA Publications GmbH & Co. Verlag KG Singapore Branch, Singapore.